# COLES NOTES

## Key Point

*Basic concepts in point form.*

## Close Up

*Additional hints, notes, tips or background information.*

## Watch Out!

*Areas where problems frequently occur.*

## Quick Tip

*Concise ideas to help you learn what you need to know.*

## Remember This!

*Essential material for mastery of the topic.*

## Your Guide to ...

# Wilderness Survival

**Emergency shelter**

**Fire, water & first aid**

**Camping & trail tips**

COLES NOTES have been an indispensable aid to students on five continents since 1948.

COLES NOTES now offer titles on a wide range of general interest topics as well as traditional academic subject areas and individual literary works. All COLES NOTES are written by experts in their fields and reviewed for accuracy by independent authorities and the Coles Editorial Board.

COLES NOTES provide clear, concise explanations of their subject areas. Proper use of COLES NOTES will result in a broader understanding of the topic being studied. For academic subjects, COLES NOTES are an invaluable aid for study, review and exam preparation. For literary works, COLES NOTES provide interesting interpretations and evaluations which supplement the text but are not intended as a substitute for reading the text itself. Use of the NOTES will serve not only to clarify the material being studied, but should enhance the reader's enjoyment of the topic.

**Cataloguing in Publication Data**
Schaber, Wally 1950–
Your guide to ... wilderness survival:
emergency shelter, fire water & first aid,
camping & trail tips

(Coles notes) ISBN 0-7740-0603-X
1. Wilderness survival – Canada. I. Title. II. Series.

GV200.5.S32 1999     613.6'9     C99-931966-3

Publisher: Nigel Berrisford
Editor: Paul Kropp
Writer: Wally Schaber

Book design: Karen Petherick
Layout and illustration: Christine Cullen

Printed and bound in Canada by Webcom Limited
Cover finish : Webcom's Exclusive DURACOAT

# Contents

Introduction  **Wilderness and wilderness survival**                                  1

Chapter 1  **Survival – priorities and behavior**                                  4
           *Mental toughness*
           *Increasing the survival odds: seven steps*

Chapter 2  **First aid**                                                          10
           *First-aid ABCs*
           *Secondary treatment*
           *Cold weather issues*
           *First-aid kits*

Chapter 3  **Shelter**                                                            19
           *Campsite selection*
           *Emergency shelters*
           *Types of shelters*
           *Winter shelters*
           *Other natural shelters*

Chapter 4  **Fire, water, food**                                                  28
           *Fire*
           *Difficult fire situations*
           *Water*
           *Water facts and tips*
           *Food*
           *Modern trail meals*
           *Organizing your menu and packing*
           *The wannigan*

**Chapter 5**   **Clothing**                                          **45**
*How to dress for outdoor activities*
*Emergency clothing*


**Chapter 6**   **Wings, fangs, claws and poison**                    **50**
*Reptiles*
*Insects*
*Poisonous plants*
*Carnivores*


**Chapter 7**   **Weather, navigation and self-rescue**               **56**
*Before you leave*
*While travelling*
*Finding north: four techniques*
*Weather*
*Predicting weather*
*Emergency signals*


**Chapter 8**   **Leadership and group behavior**                     **65**
*Participating in a commercial or private expedition*


**Chapter 9**   **Wilderness connoisseur**                            **69**
*Wilderness preservation groups*


**Appendix 1**   **Glossary**                                         **74**


**Appendix 2**   **Suggested reading**                                **78**

# Wilderness and wilderness survival

Only three generations ago, most Canadians lived in a rural setting, living and working on the land. Your great-grandparents probably had daily contact with the natural environment and depended on water, crops and livestock for survival. Their parents spent a significant amount of time teaching them about the land: how to travel through it, harvest it, care for it and enjoy its natural beauty.

Today's society gives greater value to other skills. If you choose, it's possible to avoid any contact with wilderness. City life cuts many of us off from significant contact with any truly natural environment – and leaves us ill-equipped to tackle the wilderness on our own.

While the dictionary defines wilderness as a "barren, uninhabitable, confusing, inhospitable environment," each of us has our own definition of wilderness, depending on where that "barren, uninhabitable, confusing" boundary begins in our mind. As Margaret Atwood wrote so convincingly in *Survival*, the idea of wilderness is central to Canadian literature and to the Canadian psyche, even if most of us choose to live in metropolitan areas.

These days, more and more Canadians are feeling a call to experience wilderness in one form or another. Camping and "adventure travel" are two of the fastest-growing sectors of our tourism market. We continue to take pride in our link to wilderness through art, writing, films … and summer holidays. Often, the wilderness presented in these vacation spots is tamed by the tour or camp organizers and by modern technology.

Nonetheless, floods, ice storms, avalanches and forest fires still require Canadians to cope with natural emergencies. These events demand survival skills that might have been second-nature 100 years ago, but require special attention today. Sometimes, too, our modern modes of transport break down, leaving us stranded, or worse, in environments where we must adapt immediately to survive.

It was the American psychologist Abraham Maslow who first categorized a human hierarchy of needs. Maslow suggested that a person's needs, in order, are:

**Biological** – air, water, food, shelter, sex, sleep

**Safety** – protection from the elements, disease, fear

**Love and belonging**

**Esteem** – self-esteem and esteem of others

**Cognitive** – knowledge, meaning, inquiry, order

**Aesthetic** – beauty, balance, form

**Self-actualization** – realization of one's potential

Although there is no doubt that a successful survival scenario in an emergency would demand all your skills to satisfy your biological and safety needs, survival experts agree that the other needs are also vital. Strong bonds of love and belonging, for instance, maintain your will to live.

Many needs, including esteem, cognitive and aesthetic, can be fulfilled on a well-planned wilderness vacation, that allows you to explore with friends the beauty and challenges of travelling through pristine wilderness.

These notes are designed to help you travel through two wilderness scenarios. The first assumes you are entering the wilderness **willingly** – so you can prepare for an enjoyable experience by carrying your own shelter, food, clothing, navigation tools and first-aid kit. The second scenario assumes you are encountering the wilderness due to **some uncontrollable circumstance** – you become lost or isolated in a wilderness environment with minimal equipment and must rely on your own resources to survive.

In most circumstances, the wilderness is a habitable, reasonably safe and beautiful environment. Indeed, Canada has some of the most spectacular wilderness in the world. With the tips in these notes, you should feel more comfortable exploring our country's natural wildernesses – and more confident in your abilities to survive should some problem occur.

Reading about these skills is one step toward learning wilderness survival – but wilderness trips with professional guides are a better approach to developing these skills. In an emergency, you need survival skills that are second-nature to you – and this book may not be close at hand.

# CHAPTER ONE

# Survival – priorities and behavior

Every adult has some experience of being thrust into "a barren, uninhabitable, confusing environment." Think back to your first day at school, an unexpected walk in the dark, or some wary navigation through a strange city. Did you panic, run, get angry, depressed or quit? Of course not. You did what all of us do in difficult situations – you found a way to calm yourself and seek common-sense solutions to the problems at hand.

A great deal of survival success, in any scenario, depends on your ability to control your mind and develop mental toughness. Fear and panic lead to an enormous waste of energy. In the wilderness, this often results in a misdirected flight path (most often a circle). And in a group survival situation, panic leads to anger, dissension and conflict.

Sitting down and applying common sense in evaluating your situation is the essential first step in any survival and rescue effort.

### MENTAL TOUGHNESS

Most rescues occur within one to three days of the discovery that a person is missing (hence the importance of letting someone know when you're going into the wilderness and when you expect to come out). If you are like most Canadians, you have already "stored" enough calories on your body to easily survive three days **without any food**. Given the ample water found in most of Canada's wilderness areas, and the minimal danger from wildlife, what is the major threat in a survival situation? **The major threat is a lack of mental toughness that drives our will to survive.**

Most casualties of wilderness emergencies die from giving up.

Afterwards, it often turns out that shelter was close, water within hearing distance, food readily at hand – but the victim just seemed to give up. Your will to live is essential to finding solutions, reduce pain, ignoring discomfort, minimizing boredom, provide leadership and increasing patience.

While neither a book nor a wilderness course can teach mental toughness, survivors of life-threatening wilderness experiences have talked about mental tricks that helped them survive:

- how important a photograph in their wallet was to them
- how they focused on three things they were going to do when they got home
- how they kept a vision, song or joke shared with a loved one foremost in their minds

Remember that Maslow's third need – a feeling of love and belonging – is a key element in human survival. Water, food, medical treatment – all these can be found or delayed, but your mind set requires immediate attention.

Ninety-five percent of all wilderness survivors have two characteristics in common:
the will to live and common sense.

### INCREASING THE SURVIVAL ODDS: SEVEN STEPS

Okay, maybe it won't happen to you. You'll never be in an airplane accident, have your car break down in the country, go for a walk and get lost, get forced to detour into unknown territory by a forest fire, get caught in a flood, have to deal with an avalanche, angry bear....

**Unfortunately, there are thousands of stories on record of people like you being forced to rely on survival skills – overnight or longer.**

Why not increase your odds for survival, or at least your comfort level, by learning some basic survival skills? It's wise to invest a little study in the basics before you have to deal with survival scenarios in real life.

Here are seven steps to improving your odds in a survival situation.

### Step 1 – control

Sit down and gain control of your emotions and your immediate strategy. Everyone gets lost sooner or later. Accidents happen. Don't waste energy on being angry and running desperately after a quick solution. If you are in a group, appoint a logical leader. If you are alone, congratulations! You've been elected leader unanimously.

### Step 2 – first aid

Is anyone seriously hurt?

Once you've got control of yourself, you are ready to apply common-sense first-aid. Stop the bleeding, deal with the shock, deal with the outside temperature. (Chapter 2 gives details on all this.)

### Step 3 – shelter

How exposed are you? How much daylight is left? You do not want to lose precious energy to wind, cold, rain or excessive sunlight. If you are exposed or you have less than half a day's light left, begin immediately to establish the best, closest shelter. (There's more on this in Chapter 3.)

### Step 4 – make a plan

If time allows, do this as step 3. Otherwise do your planning in the comfort of your shelter.

To begin, build your confidence by taking an inventory of the tools and knowledge at your disposal. Empty your pack and pockets to identify what could be useful:

**Fire starter** – matches, lighter, magnifying glass, steel
**Hunting tools** – laces, wire, rope, belt, jewelry, pins, tinfoil, knife
**For signals and navigation** – watch, pen, pencil, reflective material
**For energy and pain relief** – medicines and food sources
**For shelter and warmth** – clothing, anything waterproof, bug-proof or sunproof

After your physical inventory is complete, start on your knowledge inventory. If you have the means to write, this will immediately give you a sense of better control of your situation.

- Make a map.
- Start a diary.
- Who knows you are here? When will they report you missing?
- Where are you – generally? Are there any major landmarks to look for?
- What else do you know, or can guess, about your situation?

### *Step 5 – stay put*

Do not move more than the radius you can see from your resting spot. Anyone looking for you will begin where you are right now.

Move to the closest, best source of shelter *within sight*. Then establish your overnight shelter and source of firewood, bedding and water. If you are close to a vehicle, and it is safe, use the vehicle as your shelter.

### *Step 6 – three-day camp*

The next morning, re-evaluate your shelter based on information gathered from a higher vantage point. Remember, your rescuers will be looking for you in an organized grid pattern. You do not want to make their search more difficult by being a moving target. Within the immediate area (within shouting distance), evaluate your situation for a three-day stay.

- Is there a better source of shelter, food and water?
- Is there a site where you can watch for help and rescuers can see you?
- Is there an area where you can set up your signal for help?
- Your current location might be fine, but more likely you'll find better quarters a short distance away. Move to the better site and stay put for 72 hours!

Most rescues are accomplished within **three days**. Only a handful of individuals ever have to survive in the wilderness for a week or a month before they finally straggle out to civilization. If you stay put for three days, there's a 90-percent chance that someone will come to your rescue. But if you decide to wander around, better learn to enjoy the scenery.

### *Step 7 – self-rescue*

At some point, you will know you must move – for food, because the search planes have stopped, you need to seek help for an injured party, you're bored, your confidence is crumbling – whatever the reason. After waiting a logical amount of time, usually three days, wait one more day while you plan your strategy.

## Wilderness wallet

You wouldn't think of going into the city without a wallet full of urban survival gear: credit cards, cash, medical card, subway map. Why not exercise the same strategy when going into the wild?

Design a wilderness wallet to fit into your pocket and get used to sliding it into your chest or hip pocket **every day of every trip – no matter how short or long**.

Prepare a larger wilderness wallet for your car, boat or suitcase. Ideally the wilderness wallet should be a small, waterproof, multifunctional container (like a candy tin which could double as a cup). Suggested contents are:

- fish hooks, 6 m (20 ft.) line
- lighter
- "strike anywhere" matches (in a waterproof container)
- small compass
- 6 m (20 ft.) snare wire
- Tylenol 3 tablets (10)
- water purification tablets (10)
- personal medicine
- small pencil
- family photo (taped in lid of container)
- safety pins
- dental floss
- needle
- #10 scalpel
- small tube of crazy glue
- small Swiss army knife
- Oxo cubes (4)

Later you'll see how all of these can be useful in different survival situations.

# CHAPTER TWO

# First aid

In any emergency situation, the first priority is to get enough control of yourself and your emotions so that you can help others without worsening their situation or endangering yourself. In a plane or car crash, for instance, be certain that you can see straight and think straight before you try to be a hero.

Then, proceed logically:

- Evacuate all non-injured people first.
- Stabilize the environment. Deal with actual or threatened fire, avalanche, unbalanced vehicle, etc.
- Do not move victims with a life-threatening injury or anyone with a back or neck injury *unless this is absolutely necessary* (immediate danger of fire, for instance). Other victims can be moved to where treatment can more sensibly be provided.
- Apply first aid to those who would benefit from it. Protect yourself, if possible, with rubber gloves from the first aid kit before applying treatments.

It is absolutely critical that you not increase the danger or anxiety for victims, yourself or the uninjured members of the party by rushing to their aid before gaining control of your senses and the environment.

### FIRST-AID THE ABCS

For life-threatening injuries, professionals rank the priorities using the ABC rule.

**A for airway** You must get air into the victim's lungs and circulate the oxygen through the blood stream **fast**. An unconscious victim will often have the tongue blocking the air passage (also check for liquids, food). Take action. Roll the victim carefully onto the back, supporting the neck and spine. Tilt the head, pull the tongue forward if necessary, then clear the passage. To apply A.R. (artificial respiration) or mouth-to-mouth resuscitation, cover the victim's mouth with yours, pinch the nose and blow hard – twice (use a mouth-to-mouth shield if available in your kit). Continue this process until the victim is revived. Check for a pulse. If not present combine with C below.

**B for bleeding** Extreme bleeding must be stopped immediately with direct pressure! Use a large compress bandage or clean cloth and hand pressure. If this does not work, apply a tourniquet. A tourniquet can be made of any flat material that will not cut the skin, like a belt, applied above the wound. The tourniquet is twisted around the limb until its pressure cuts off blood circulation and blood loss.

A tourniquet must be loosened slowly every half-hour. If pressure alone controls the bleeding at that time, do not reapply the tourniquet.

**C for CPR** CPR is applied alternatively with the techniques in A (above) if the victim has no pulse. To check for a pulse, place your middle and index fingers on the large vein near the neck muscle, next to the Adam's apple. Allow a full minute to locate a pulse as it may be faint if the individual is in shock or has gotten cold.

If there is no pulse, begin CPR (see illustration) by kneeling at 90 degrees to the victim's chest. Locate the breastbone (between the ribs, up 5 cm/2 in.). With stiff arms, elbows together, cross your fingers palms down; then compress the breastbone smoothly 2-4 cm (1-2 in.) with the heel of your lower hand and stiff arms. Continue this at a smooth rhythm of 80-100 compressions per minute. Remember to take a smooth pause at the return phase of the rising breastbone.

If CPR is to be combined with mouth-to-mouth resuscitation by an assistant, pause every fifth compression to allow two mouth-to-mouth breaths. If you are working alone, pause every tenth compression and switch to the mouth-to-mouth position for two breaths.

If CPR is going to work, it will usually succeed in 15-30 minutes. Stop CPR immediately when the heartbeat and breathing return.

After applying the ABCs, treat all victims for shock and hypothermia by insulating them from the air and ground. Keep any victims lying down. You can improve circulation to their body core by loosening clothing and elevating their legs slightly if appropriate (if there are no broken bones).

**This is not a first-aid book.** We are only attempting to give you a sense of how to prioritize your situation. You must seek professional training for effective CPR and mouth-to-mouth resuscitation techniques; Heimlich manoeuvre (for choking victims); and advanced wilderness first-aid techniques. Such courses are offered regularly in larger cities. Check with:

- St. John Ambulance
- Red Cross
- youth groups – Boy Scouts, Girl Guides, Cadets, Venturers
- outdoor specialty stores
- community colleges and school boards
- community centers
- your union or workplace

## SECONDARY TREATMENT

- **Do** clean all minor wounds gently with soap and water (ideally warm water) and dress with a sterile bandage.
- **Do** check daily for signs of infection (redness, swelling, pus, fever) and change the dressing after cleaning a wound.
- **Do** talk to the victim regularly and watch for signs of shock, discomfort and unusual behavior that may indicate internal injuries or hypothermia.
- **Don't** move victims with back, neck or life-threatening injuries unless absolutely necessary. If necessary, create a back and neck brace support for transport.
- **Don't** try to set broken bones unless it is necessary to stop bleeding (but do create traction to protect the break from movement and shocks.)
- **Don't** remove impaled objects – bleeding may result. Isolate with cushioning and support.
- **Don't** give liquids to victims with suspected internal injuries if evacuation is likely to happen quickly. Liquid on the lips will ease thirst just as well.
- **Don't make matters worse by providing incorrect treatment. Your common sense and natural instinct to comfort the victim is often the best medical attention you can provide.**

## COLD WEATHER ISSUES

Cold weather and snow complicate the application of first aid because shelter, evacuation and water may not be as readily available. Cold conditions will also hamper you, the aid giver, and accelerate the victim's need for treatment. Therefore, winter demands extra caution and urgency. Again, protect yourself first from the effects of cold and the way it can impair your judgment and ability to help others.

Two cold weather conditions deserve special discussion.

### Frostbite

Frostbite is more accurately described as the freezing of your extremities. When deprived of heat, water or energy, your body will reduce the flow of blood to the skin and tips of your limbs (fingers, toes, cheeks, ears, nose) to protect vital organs. This reduced blood flow can lead to white and frozen tissue (frostbite).

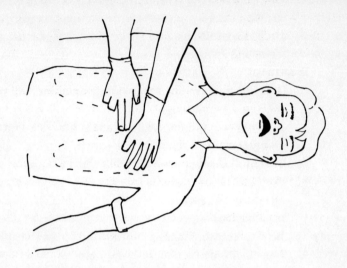

**CPR hand placement, adult**

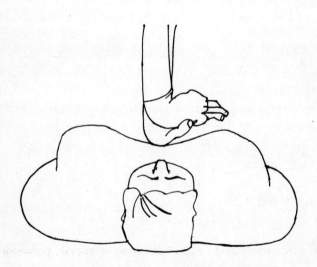

**CPR hand position, adult**

Frostbite is preceded by frostnip (a reddening, then whitening of the extremity that has not yet frozen hard). **Frostnip** may be treated by placing the extremity next to warm skin (under arms, in groin, on the stomach). **Frostbite** requires *gradual* reheating of the extremity in warm water (see below).

**Treatment**

- **Don't** begin reheating frostbitten extremities until you are safely in a permanent shelter. Frostbite will not get worse once you're out of the cold – unless you reheat the extremity and then freeze it again.
- **Don't** rub frostbite with anything – including snow.
- **Don't** reheat the frostbite by a fire or stove or with chemical-heat packs.
- **Do** immerse the affected areas in water at 40°C (104°F) for 30-60 minutes. Blistering and sensitivity will occur. After thawing the tissue, treat it the way you would a burn with gauze and antiseptic ointment.

## *Hypothermia*

This is not a winter-only danger! Hypothermia can occur in any season with conditions that take heat away from the body faster than the body can maintain normal core temperatures. The loss of 1-10°C (3-20°F) of body core temperature results in symptoms that range from shivering, to loss of speech, to loss of motor skills, to unconsciousness.

How does the body lose heat? Your body can be robbed of heat in these ways:

- directly through transfer of heat to colder air or water
- directly to a solid object (ground, aluminum boat, pole or paddle)
- by moving air (wind chill) or your own motion (running)
- through evaporation off skin (sweat)

The best approach to hypothermia is, of course, prevention. How can you retain or generate heat?

- Wear hats, mitts, gloves (more than 50 percent of heat loss is through the extremities).

- Dress in layers – with the layer next to your skin made of artificial non-absorbent fibers (not cotton) that wick moisture away from the skin.
- Sit on a closed cell pad (not the ground or an aluminum seat).
- Wear windproof clothing.
- Eat and drink lots of high-energy foods and liquids.
- Keep moving.

**Treatment**
- **Do** address the source of heat loss – remove wet clothes, put on a hat and mitts, do not lie on the ground, move out of the wind into a sheltered area.
- **Do** assist the victim's ability to generate heat. Give the person dry clothes, put the victim in a sleeping bag or put a sleeping pad underneath them. It's possible to transfer your body heat to the victim with skin-to-skin contact inside a sleeping bag or parka.
- **Do** give the victim high-energy food and warm, sugar-laced drinks. Use flavored gelatin mix, honey or sugar in warm water.

In extreme cases of hypothermia (the victim has fallen into icy water and is unconscious), professional skills and hot baths are required. The victim's heartbeat will be very faint in these circumstances. Beware of heart failure from quick, extreme changes. CPR may be required.

## *FIRST-AID KITS*

All first-aid kits are not created equal – and the best is the one you create for yourself. In building your wilderness first-aid kit, as opposed to what you can purchase for home use at the drugstore, you should consider the possible uses it may have to deal with:

- How long do you expect to be in the wilderness?
- How large is your group?

- How skilled is the primary first-aid giver in the group?
- What special situations does your route offer (water, cold, heat, animals, etc.)?
- What prerequisites does your group demand of the kit (pre-existing illnesses, allergies, etc.)?

**Container** When you need to use the kit, you want it to stay open, stay organized, and for the contents to be easily accessible. While you're travelling, you want the kit to be waterproof, shockproof and packable. You may choose to combine a soft, roll-open "organizer kit" with a hard box or cylinder for waterproofing.

Remember to place your kit in the *same* outside pocket of your pack – and let everyone in the group know *where it is and where it belongs*. When you most need the kit, you'll have the least time to go looking for it.

The most qualified first-aid giver should control the kit. On a long trip, encourage a daily "open for business" session to treat blisters, aches and pains before they develop into serious problems. Someone should also have the responsibility of replenishing the kit's supplies when your trip is finished.

**Contents** Given all the variables we've mentioned, you should mentally organize your kit's contents into four categories. Pick and choose from this list (for a group of four hiking in temperate climates), depending on your projected needs:

| Tools | Quantity |
|---|---|
| blunt-nose medical scissors | 1 |
| #11 sterile-wrapped scalpel | 2 |
| large safety pins | 6 |
| dental floss | 1 |
| splint (aluminum/foam) | 1 |
| thermometer | 1 |
| tweezers | 1 |
| barrier surgical gloves (avoid latex due to allergies) | 4 pair |
| CPR microshield | 1 |
| pencil, notepad, matches | 1 each |
| irrigating syringe | 1 |

reference book (recommended: *Wilderness and Travel Medicine*)

## Bandage materials

pressure pads . . . . . . . . . . . . . . . . . . . . . . . . . . . . . . . . . . .4

sterile squares (assorted sizes) . . . . . . . . . . . . . . . . . . . . . .12

gauze rolls, 2 cm x 10 m . . . . . . . . . . . . . . . . . . . . . . . . . . .2

non-adherent dressing for burns . . . . . . . . . . . . . . .small box

elastic bandage for sprains . . . . . . . . . . . . . . . . . . . . . . . . .1

wound closure strips . . . . . . . . . . . . . . . . . . . . . . . . . . . .box

moleskin for blisters . . . . . . . . . . . . . . . . . . . . . . . .small roll

cleansing pads with antiseptic . . . . . . . . . . . . . . . . . . . . . .12

triangular bandage for slings . . . . . . . . . . . . . . . . . . . . . . . .1

## Creams and ointments

cortisporin ophthalmic ointment . . . . . . . . . . . . . .small tube

aloe vera gel (for burns, frostbite) . . . . . . . . . . . . . .small tube

providone iodine solution . . . . . . . . . . . . . . . . . .small bottle

Vaseline . . . . . . . . . . . . . . . . . . . . . . . . . . . . . . . .small tube

polysporin ointment . . . . . . . . . . . . . . . . . . . . . . .small tube

tinactin ointment (for fungus) . . . . . . . . . . . . . . . . . . . .tube

## Non-prescription internal medicines

*Caution must be used in administering any medicine. Read the labels! Check with your doctor or pharmacist for a variety of fresh non-prescription drugs to treat:*

constipation/diarrhea
headache
mild muscle/joint inflammation
sinus, nasal congestion
hayfever, mild allergies
allergic reaction to beesting
toothache

You might also want to include some **antibiotics** for infections, though these must be ordered by prescription from a doctor. Penicillin is a standby, but a significant portion of the population is allergic to the drug. Popular substitutes include erythromycin and ampicillin. Participants on a trip who require **prescription drugs** as personal medication should bring a supply and advise the principal first-aid giver at the outset what medications they take or require.

# CHAPTER THREE

# Shelter

If you are carrying your shelter on your back or in your canoe, you are going to want to select a shelter that provides you with protection from sun, wind, rain, snow and bugs. You'll want all this without adding excessive weight to your pack. A nylon tarp is one option but this provides little protection from insects. Modern, lightweight tents come in many shapes and include countless design features you may or may not require.

Bikers, hikers and kayakers concentrate on compactness and weight-to-size ratio. Well-built one- and two-person tents weigh from one to two kilograms (three to five pounds). Canoeists who can afford the luxury of carrying a little more weight will select a two- to four-person tent weighing three kilograms or more (6 to 10 pounds). Dome-shaped tents with three or four poles offer better wind resistance (at the expense of ventilation) than rectangular or A-frame tents.

The better tents on the market today offer these 10 key features:

1. separate fly (roof), tent body and poles
2. aircraft aluminum poles, shock-corded together
3. PSI (pounds per square inch) waterproof coating on the floor, side walls and fly
4. breathable rip-stop nylon body
5. no-seeum (the smallest) nylon netting in the doors and windows
6. good plastic zippers (#6+) in one or two doors
7. a method of separating the fly from the tent body (pole sleeves or hooks) to allow maximum ventilation
8. complete coverage of the door, windows and tent body by

the fly, without touching the tent in any area (held out by pegs and guylines)

9. sealed/welded seams in the fly and floor at any stitched area
10. a protective coating on the fly to prevent ultraviolet rays from affecting the nylon

On your wilderness trip, you will be spending one-third of your time in your tent. Purchase a tent with as many of these key features as you can afford so you will be comfortable. A reliable shelter is the first priority in any wilderness situation. Staying warm and dry – and enjoying a good night's sleep – are the keys to an enjoyable holiday (or successful self-rescue).

## Nylon tent

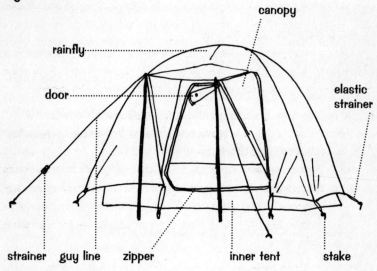

## CAMPSITE SELECTION

Whether you are using a tent for camping or making an emergency shelter, try to find as many of the following features in your campsite as possible:

- level site for your shelter and kitchen
- good water supply
- wind and weather protection (should include shade)
- dry ground (good drainage, avoid a flood plain)
- no insect nests or obvious animal trails
- no poison ivy or other allergenic plants
- no natural hazards (hanging branches, deadfalls, rock slides, avalanches, tides)

And remember, an eco-responsible camper will try to avoid naturally sensitive areas, especially during spawning and nesting periods.

## EMERGENCY SHELTERS

In an emergency situation, finding or constructing shelter is a top priority. The quality and location of your shelter depends on your evaluation of the situation as discussed in Chapter 2. To review:

1. If you are travelling, allow adequate time to find shelter.
2. If bad weather is threatening, invest more time in weather-proofing your shelter.
3. If you are waiting for help to arrive, then invest as much time and energy as required to gain reliable shelter from the elements.
4. Remember to locate near a site that allows for signalling aircraft.

## TYPES OF SHELTERS

Sometimes even the best tent can't keep you as comfortable as what your natural environment offers. Especially in emergency situations, it's vital to know how nature can supply the best protection from the elements.

**Rock and river** Often a cliff or dry river bank will offer a natural overhang that will make, with minimal effort and a reflector fire, an excellent shelter. Check the site for animal "tenants" and structural strength, then select a cooking area and sleeping area. Build a fireplace with wind protection, and make sure the smoke will clear the mouth of the shelter. Collect a large supply of dry firewood. Build your fire to heat and dry the space while you gather evergreen boughs (available in much of Canada) for your bed. The boughs act as insulation, and a slow-burning fire will keep you warm and comfortable all night.

**Conical shelters** *Teepee (made with skins) or wickiup (made with vegetation)* This classic native shelter has been home to nomadic people for centuries. Lash three 3 m (10 ft.) poles in a tripod with any available laces or roots. Spread the legs to form a 2.5 m (8 ft.) circle, then stand a series of similar poles around the tripod to form the frame. Now weave any available material horizontally through the frame (boughs, cattails, grass, sod, bark) until your shelter is windproof.  Add additional mud and packing material to cracks for waterproofing. Another layer of poles on the outside may be required for windproofing during very bad weather.  A fire may be built on the lee side where your door is also located.

## Pole wickiup

POLE
DUFF
GRASS
POLE

**Lean-to** If you are travelling and not in need of an elaborate shelter, you may discover a basic natural frame for a three-sided shelter. A large overturned tree, root or windfall can provide two-thirds of your shelter. Simply add windbreaks to the side and roof, build your fireplace at the mouth and your bough bed at the low end.

## Lean-to shelter

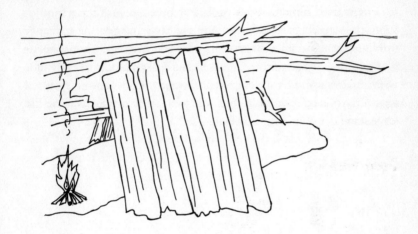

While modern tents offer considerable advantages in dealing with the elements – quick set up, reliable waterproofing, effective insect control – traditional shelters can also provide very effective protection. The Inuit igloo, for instance, when lit with a tiny oil lamp (the *kudlik* dates from prehistoric times), not only protects its occupants from Arctic winds and -40°C temperatures outside, it will warm overnight to a temperature comfortably over the freezing mark. If you have a seal skin on which to sleep, you'll find this ancient shelter far more effective than most modern tents in an Arctic blizzard.

Always be careful to clear combustible material away from your firepit. Build your fire on stone or sand with 50 cm (20 in.) non-combustible reflector/spark catcher in back, and no combustible material for 1 m (3 ft.) to the sides and 2 m (6 ft.) above.

## WINTER SHELTERS

Winter camping is a unique and beautiful experience much more challenging than summer camping. Your number-one challenge will be balancing your internal thermostat! When you are working and generating your own heat, you'll find you need surprisingly little additional insulation. Your biggest challenge will be wicking away the moisture you generate to prevent heat loss due to evaporation next to your skin.

At times of rest, however, you will need extensive layers of insulation and windproofing. (see Chapter 5). Winter tents must be constructed with special features not found in summer tents, to deal with the following special problems:

**Wind** Often in winter, campsites are associated with ski and snowshoe trails that take advantage of lakes, swamps and mountain ridges. The forests are also less dense without their summer foliage – therefore wind is a more significant factor.

**Snow/ice load** Winter precipitation can form heavy loads. Your tent must support and shed this load effectively.

**Frozen ground** You cannot peg out your tent in the winter. You must rely on a snow flap (a piece of material sewn along the outside floor or fly, on which you pile snow) to weigh down your tent or long guylines extending out from the fly to be tied to trees and "snow anchors" (special snow pegs, sticks or rocks you bury in the snow).

**Other considerations** Choose a bright color (yellow, orange, red) so your tent is easily spotted in an emergency. Size does matter: select a tent with more room rather than less. Winter gear is bulky and sleeping in a group is warmer than sleeping alone.

Winter tents can become nearly airtight sealed in a blanket of snow, so ventilation and exits are very important in the winter. Metal zippers freeze. Your tent should have lubricated nylon zippers and zipper pulls that can be operated with mitts on. Aluminum poles with shock cord (an elastic cord that connects all the units of each section together) are a must. As well, an extended conical vestibule at one end allows room for a stove, a storage and boot removal area, and adds an additional windbreak.

If you're going shopping, you'll probably find that the ideal winter mountain tent is two-door, yellow or orange, with four aluminum poles and aerodynamic dome with a fly including vestibule, with extra long guylines and snow anchors. Now all you have to do is explain that to the salesperson.

## OTHER NATURAL SHELTERS

**Snow caves** If you are in an area where snow falls or drifts to a sufficient depth and density (about two to three metres of heavy snow), you can carve out a snow cave. Snow knives (machete-style) and snow shovels are useful tools, but in an emergency any flat stick or strong flat surface (bark, stone, ice) will do.

Dig along the base of the drift, creating a tunnel 1 m (3 ft.) long and 1 m (3 ft.) wide. Now begin your tunnel toward the center of the drift at 45 degrees to create an entrance to the cave higher than your ground-level entrance. From this point, expand your cave in a dome shape, leaving a minimum wall thickness of 70 cm (28 in.). Place sticks of this length through the top to gauge the depth of the snow. Smooth out the inner walls, and drill a hole through to the surface for ventilation.

The main cave is your sleeping area. Any warm air will be trapped in this area and your sleeping bag and/or emergency bough bed will provide insulation. Temperatures in a snow cave will remain constant – near 0˚C – no matter what the temperature is outside. It can get even warmer when heated by your body or by additional heat from a candle.

# Snow cave

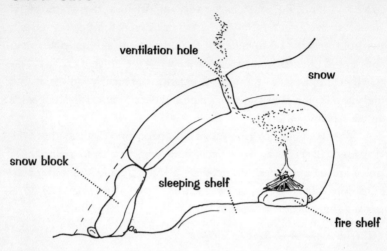

**Quinzie** If the snow in your area is not of sufficient depth or is too soft, then you will have to create the texture and depth you need. Begin by piling up the snow to a sufficient height and waiting for it to sinter (harden and bond). Create a 2-3 m (6-9 ft.) mound by shovelling snow with any tool possible. Smooth (don't pack) your dome. Then let it sit for two to three hours (less time is needed in extremely cold weather).

When you are ready to hollow out your dome, poke three or four 30 cm (12 in.) marker sticks into the top to prevent you from hollowing out the walls to unsafe thickness. Repeat the snow cave procedure, with the exception of the door tunnel. For maximum space inside, dig your door tunnel straight in at the level of the frozen ground. Remember to ventilate your quinzie properly. Close your door with a pack, snow block or other object that does not completely seal off the airflow.

**In emergencies** Snow caves and quinzies take a lot of time and energy to build, two things that might be in short supply in an emergency. If this is the case, simply create a rectangular trench big enough to accommodate two people, with enough space for you to stretch out and not touch the sides. Cover the floor with anything that will insulate. Find something to make a roof (a tarp, snow-covered boughs, snow blocks, your pack). Pile snow around three edges of your roof and crawl in, closing the fourth side as well as possible but still allowing ventilation. This shelter isn't fancy, but it can save your life in an emergency.

The Inuit igloo, of course, is the most-efficient snow shelter ever developed. Unfortunately, it requires skills, snow conditions and experience beyond the scope of these notes. If you get a chance to travel in the Arctic, you can get lessons in building an igloo. The Inuit can assemble a good-size igloo in about two hours, but given enough practice you and a friend might be able to assemble one in an afternoon. An overnight spent in an igloo, heated and illuminated only by a *kudlik* (oil candle) while sleeping on a seal skin is a uniquely Canadian experience.

 Practice building these shelters near a heated cabin *before* your have to rely on surviving in one in a wilderness situation.

# CHAPTER FOUR

# Fire, water, food

In order of priority, warmth and water always take precedence over food. You can survive for three days without any food at all, but in a wilderness situation you might be frozen or dehydrated by then. So let's consider these essentials in order.

### FIRE

Fire provides warmth, comfort and protection. A fire permits cooking and can be your major rescue signal (smoke). If you have a source for starting fires (matches, lighter, magnifying glass), protect it carefully. Once you start a fire, keep it going 24 hours a day with coals. If you need to be rescued, keep handy quick kindling and green boughs for creating smoke. It takes a lot of smoke to be seen from 1,000 feet in the air.

Three fires (or three of anything) in a triangle is the universal signal for help!

**Elements of a good fire** Even with matches, you do not want to use more than one match to light your fire. Take extra care in setting up. Visualize a pyramid of materials beginning with the small, 30-second flame from your match and ending with a pile of hardwood burning merrily. Each level of materials must catch its flame from the level below and burn with enough energy to ignite the heavier layer above. Make sure there is enough air circulation so that oxygen can reach your burning material – but not so much wind that it blows out the fire.

**Tinder** This is your finest, lightest material. It may be ignited from a match, spark or intensified heat from the sun. Tinder is shredded material (paper, bark, grass, dry moss, dry plants, nest material, softwood shavings) gathered into a ball or nest to accept the match.

**Kindling** Tinder will ignite softwood kindling the size of a pencil. The best kindling is the dry twigs at the base of spruce and other coniferous trees.

**Breakable wood** Dried limbs and deadwood you can break with your hands and knees is the core supply of firewood available without an axe.

**Softwood** Evergreens, especially cedar, burn faster and brighter than hardwoods.

**Hardwood** Deciduous trees like maple, birch and oak, burn longer and hotter and make better coals.

**Greenwood** Live trees will eventually burn but are best used for your bedding.

## Ten fire-building tips

1.  If you find a good supply of tinder, make extra tinder balls for wet days or travelling.
2.  You do not have to break every piece of wood. Feed pieces into the fire slowly or burn wood through the middle.
3.  A tube or hollow stem is useful for blowing oxygen into coals for rekindling a fire (hose, straw, piece of rolled-up birch bark).
4.  Avoid safety matches that strike only against their own matchbox cover; carry "strike anywhere" wooden matches.
5.  Commercial gels and solid cubes of fuel are excellent fire-starter "cheaters," especially in winter.
6.  A candle you light from your match will allow you more time to ignite your kindling, as well as warm your hands and light the environment.
7.  Tinder inside a teepee of kindling is a proven means of starting a fire. Leave room for ventilation by the wind or your blowing.
8.  Build your fire against a natural rock reflector or build a reflector out of green wrist-sized logs staked into the ground behind your fire.
9.  Coals can be maintained overnight by covering them with ashes and a *thin* layer of earth to prevent the wind from burning them cold.
10. Locate the fire so that the wind carries the smoke away from your shelter but the heat is close enough to reflect into your sleeping area. Beware of your fire burning into roots and humus. Pit your fire with sand or rocks.

## DIFFICULT FIRE SITUATIONS

**In winter** Compress the snow where your firepit is to be located and check for the snow load overhead (no sense starting a fire to have it snuffed out by a small avalanche). Build a platform for the fire with large green logs, then light your fire on the platform. Re-establish the base as the fire sinks it further into the snow. It's a good idea to insulate yourself from the snow as you sit around the fire. But be careful – sparks can sometimes burn clothing, which is an inelegant and dangerous way to get warm.

**Fire without matches** Matches are a relatively new invention as a means of starting a fire. Aboriginal and other early travellers demonstrated great skill and ingenuity in inventing ways to create sparks from friction or by carrying coals to relight their fires. These skills are not teachable here, unfortunately. You will need hands-on instruction and plenty of practice to build a fire by using a hand drill and bow as people do in the movies.

Two methods with which an untrained individual may have success are magnification and steel and flint.

**Magnification** Any glass may be used to successfully heat the sun's rays to ignite tinder. Several forest fires are started every year this way because of discarded bottles. In a disaster situation, you'll find glass lenses in your flashlight, binoculars, reading glasses and glass bottles.

**Steel and flint** It is likely you will have steel on your wardrobe or in your pocket (belt buckle, knife, nail file, thermos, pot, cup). Flint is any hard stone with silica, such as quartz. To get a spark, select a sharp-edged piece of flint and strike it hard – in a crossing motion – against the steel. The sparks you generate must fall into your tinder nest. As soon as smoke appears, blow or fan the tinder *gently* until the glow ignites. Practice this at home before you try to be heroic in the wild.

## WATER

Water in its liquid or solid state is in abundant supply in most wilderness areas of Canada. *Safe* water, however, may be a concern. Water can be contaminated by suspended solids, dissolved chemicals and live bacteria. All of these can be dealt with in an emergency situation.

**Suspended solids** Filter these objects through a felt hat or the finest woven clothing item you have available. Caution: You cannot filter saltwater this way.

**Dissolved chemicals** Airborne contaminants have become worldwide pollutants these days, even in the wilderness. Chemicals seeping into a water source from a dump or natural source (oil on the surface) may make certain bodies of water unsafe. Choose another source if the water looks, smells or tastes bad.

**Live bacteria** All our drinking water contains some micro-organisms, but some are more dangerous than others. Boiling water will kill most bacteria, viruses and parasites.

**Protozoa 1 – 5 microns in size** Protozoa are a potential threat in all untreated water. These micro-organisms can be spread by both humans and animals. Protozoan cysts may have a protective shell that make them resistant to iodine; therefore, protozoa are best removed by filtration. Examples: *Giardia lambli, Cryptosporidium*.

**Bacteria 0.2-0.5 microns in size** Most bacteria can be removed by filtration, but some bacteria may be small enough to pass through a standard filter and must be eliminated with a chemical disinfectant such as iodine. Boiling is also effective. Examples: *E. Coli, Salmonella, Campylobacter* and *Cholera*.

**Viruses .004 microns and smaller** Viruses are typically spread by humans and are most likely to occur in areas where there is significant human contact. Viruses must be eliminated with chemical disinfectant because they are small enough to pass through any filter. Examples: *Hepatitis A, Norwalk* and *Rotavirus*.

## WATER FACTS AND TIPS

While travelling in wildlands, especially during extremely hot or cold conditions, you may lose more than three litres of water a day to evaporation. Don't travel if you do not have or can't find adequate water.

Clear plastic can be used to gather water through evaporation from plants or cool earth below the ground surface. Wrap a bag around cut or crushed vegetation on a slight slope. Seal the bag airtight. A limited amount of water will condense on the bag and drop down to the lower end. Similarly, a piece of plastic stretched airtight across a hole (90 x 60 cm) will condense water directly on the inside.

Put a stone on the plastic to create a depression and align a cup or pot below the depression in the hole. Water will drip into the cup all day.

## Cross section of an evaporation still

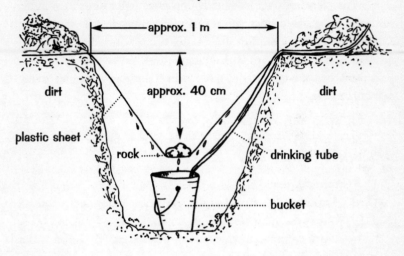

Digestion requires a lot of the body's water reserve, so don't eat until your water supply is replenished. A typical adult will drink 4-5 litres of water a day. Your body needs it. Remember, rationing water does not prolong life. Drink what you need.

- Ice produces more water than snow, when melted.
- Wetland vegetation and animal trails can lead you to water.
- Drink slowly, in small mouthfuls, if you have been deprived of water.
- Rain and dew are good sources of water.
- In dry regions, water can be found trapped in rock basins that are often higher than the water table.

# FOOD

You cannot afford to expend more energy collecting food than you will gain from eating it. You need to be constantly foraging and have several potential food sources.

## Plant sources

As a plant gatherer, your only challenge is locating, identifying and preparing the proper species of plants, nuts, berries and roots. Options for carrying, storing and mixing plants with other sources of protein need to be part of your strategy.

In Canada, some of the most logical and recognizable edible wild plants are:

### Seasonal nuts, seeds and berries

Strawberries, raspberries, acorns, wild rice, blueberries, gooseberries, currants

### Wetland plants

- Arrowhead – arrow-shaped leaf, bears spring seeds and fall tubers on the roots suitable for roasting.
- Bracken fern – provides the spring delicacy fiddleheads, but inedible at other times.
- Cattails – edible root and shoot when cooked. Head and leaves are excellent weaving material and insulation. Cattails are the wildland's most all-round useful plant.
- Bull rush – peeled stem and root core both edible raw or cooked.
- Mint – excellent hot drink or flavor. Chew the leaves.
- Watercress – may be eaten raw like a salad.
- Asparagus – spring shoots are edible raw or cooked.

### Meadow species

- Clover – Seed head a good snack, greens good as a salad.
- Thistle – tall and ugly but the peeled stem and root are edible raw or cooked.
- Plantain – yes, this lawnkeeper's horror is good to eat in the spring or used as an herb on wounds.
- Dandelion – edible as a salad or boiled for tea.
- Juniper – berries are nutritious. Boil or crush to make more palatable.

- Goldenrod – large yellow head. Seeds are good in a wild game stew. Leaves are suitable for tea.
- Burdock – Yes, the plant with burrs! Spring leaves and shoots are edible cooked. Burdock roots may be roasted.

## Animal sources

You need the protein, calories and fat that come from these non-traditional North American food sources.

*Insects* Grasshoppers, grubs, nymphs, ants, crickets, don't sound too appetizing but roasted or in a stew of roots and greens, they will provide a good source of protein. Always cook insects! If you catch more than you need immediately, use some for fish bait and roast the rest for travel food. Use a stick or pine bough as a tool to catch insects.

*Reptiles, amphibians* Frogs and snakes may be your easiest prey to catch with a sharp stick or club. You need to skin frogs and snakes, clean them, then boil or fry their meaty sections. Do not spend a lot of energy here as the edible sections are minimal.

*Fish* Any piece of wire or pin or even a bone can be turned into a hook. Go after small fish. Tinfoil, a ring, berries or insects can serve as a lure. A hook does not need to be hook shape. Tie your line into the middle of a bone or pin with two sharp ends. Bait one end and you have yourself an effective skewer hook. Use your dental floss as line and to tie the hook.

Herding fish into shallows and traps works well. Crawfish and clams are also fair game. Clean and cook all fish well. Fishing is not as energy-demanding as other forms of hunting.

*Bigger game* It is possible to kill some bigger birds and animals with a club or spear. Find a hardwood shaft about 3.5 m (10 ft.), sharpen one end by rubbing it against a rock face, then harden it in the fire. Also keep your eye out for a 1 m (3 ft.) hardwood club with a knot at one end (i.e., shillelagh) or you could notch the end and lash a stone axe head into the notch. Remember you have to carry it!

Porcupines, ptarmigans and grouse are prime targets for stone-tool hunters. Trapping small birds, rabbits and ground squirrels in snares and deadfalls is within your ability. To use the snare success-fully, you need to be able to recognize an animal's trail and understand its feeding habits. A deadfall involves the animal releasing a baited trigger that deadfalls a weight to crush the victim instantly. Countless triangular options with rocks and logs are available to hunters to design. Do not practice this, except to trigger the trap yourself as it leads to death for wild and domestic animals. Similarly, the snare strangles its victim. You are encouraged to study deadfalls and snares but only practice with them if you fully intend to eat your victim.

## MODERN TRAIL MEALS

Today's wilderness travellers have all the experience of their predecessors to call upon, combined with new innovations in dehydration and gourmet-food packaging. In any major city today, by visiting your favorite delicatessen, health food store and major food retail chain you can purchase 90 percent of your trail food. The other 10 percent can be found at an outdoor specialty store (freeze-dried foods) and a specialty butcher and baker.

A demanding wilderness trip will require 3,000-4,000 calories a day of energy for each participant. The average daily requirement in the city for an adult is 1,500-2,500 calories. You must preplan your menu, first organizing the fresh and perishable parts of the menu for the beginning of the trip and dried foods later. Hard vegetables (carrots, onions, cabbage, turnip, potatoes, etc.) can last up to two weeks if they are kept dry and allowed to breathe. Smoked or vacuum-packed meats and cheeses can last at least two weeks, especially sausages that are spiced and dried. Hard, unsliced bread will last at least a week, but you are going to want to bake your own as soon as possible.

Canned goods are heavy to carry but a great flavor and protein supplement when added to your menu. Dehydrated foods serve the same function, with less weight. These can be purchased, or you can dehydrate anything in your own oven by baking it a long time (3-6 hours) at low heat (65-95°C/150-200°F).

Traditionally, the sun was used as a dehydrator of meat (jerky) and even today, sun-dried tomatoes and a lot of other dehydrated products are easily obtained at grocery stores. Start with a tour of these stores, jotting down dried goods available to you. If you're more ambitious, look up smoke houses in the phone book and order smoked bacon, meats and fish to supplement your menu.

## *ORGANIZING YOUR MENU AND PACKING*

Before planning your menu, consult your maps and trip notes to recognize the challenges (and occasional opportunities) that will affect meal planning on your trip. Most menu planners follow these rules:

- Begin the trip with 4-6 meals of fresh food.
- Plan four types of lunches:
  - ◆ travelling lunches (quick and simple)
  - ◆ rainy-day travelling lunches (soup, grilled cheese, noodles)
  - ◆ rest-day lunches (may involve baking)
  - ◆ individual day lunches (a meal that can be split up easily for a day activity)
- Take advantage of opportunities en route (ice, berries, good fishing, food cache)
- "Pack more than less." Four-thousand calories (approximately 1 kg/2lbs.) per person per day is a *lot* of food. But ending up hungry on a trip is no fun and puts undue stress on the group.
- Flexibility is the key! Eat the meal that is most appropriate for the day (fast cooking meals on cold rainy days and more intricate meals on leisurely days).

**Planning on paper** Lay out your menu plan in detail by meal and day:

| DAY 1 | Breakfast | Lunch | Dinner | Notes |
| DAY 2 | Breakfast | Lunch | Dinner | etc. |

Calculate the volume of each item you need to buy (40 servings of oatmeal, 8 fresh oranges, etc.), then shop with your menu. Mark off with a highlighter anything you have to get elsewhere or later (this becomes your fresh food shopping list).

When you're ready, find a large work surface where you can organize all your food. Mark a large clear plastic bag for each meal, each day (B1, L1, D1). Pack all the breakfasts at one time. Do the same for lunches and dinners. Label the contents of each pack to avoid useless searching.

Remove all excess packaging but put all needed recipes inside the bag and on your menu. After a final check, put the components for each meal in an appropriate bag and squeeze out the excess air. Twist-tie or knot the top.

Pack your meal bags in your pack or barrel in ascending order with the last meal of the trip on the bottom and the first on the top. For long trips, spread the load over three or four packs to avoid dangerously heavy packs and to disperse the risk of losing your food to animals or an accident. Plan ahead of time how you are going to cache your food each night (in barrels or suspended from a tree limb, with a rope pulley).

 To get almost all the air out of packed meal bags, submerge them underwater to the twist-tie or knot area before closing.

**Menu options** Most campers are happy with nine different menu options. You can easily repeat the seven non-fresh meals on the second week of your trip. Let's consider a dozen menu options – you can pick your seven favorites for the third week of an extra long trip.

**Breakfasts** Mother was not kidding – breakfast is the most important meal of the day. If you have an early riser in your group, make sure that person knows how to get the fire and coffee going. Take a moment the night before to organize your breakfast for a quick start. Most trail breakfasts consist of:

1. a hot or cold cereal – oatmeal, Red River, seven grain, muesli, granola, cream of wheat, Cheerios, grape nuts, corn flakes
2. a fruit or juice – oranges, grapefruit, juice crystals
3. an egg option – fresh bacon and eggs for day one, powdered eggs for later (Spanish, western, cheese, mushroom omelettes) OR
   10 baked or toasted options – English muffins, French toast, American toast, pancakes, crepes, muffins, banana bread, Chelsea buns, corn bread, coffee cake, scones, raisin bread, fruit cobbler

Don't forget the breakfast staples – coffee, tea, syrup, butter, jam, marmalade, honey, peanut butter, brown sugar, cinnamon, powdered or canned milk.

Breakfast taste treats include bacon, fresh fish caught en route, yogurt, smoked ham, dried or fresh fruit, fruit in the baked goods and the cereal (raisins, apricots, currants, applesauce, cranberries).

 On cold days make an extra pot of coffee or tea at breakfast and fill a thermos for the trail.

**Lunches** Most trail lunches are a smorgasboard affair where the meal planner will lay out a collection of sandwich options and the group will graze on their personal favorites. Soup and tea are traditional hot-lunch beverages.

For rest days, you may wish to plan a full-dinner lunch. Only lay out the items you want eaten. The base may be any of the following: pita, bagels (early in the trip), rye bread, compressed pumpernickel breads, hard crackers, trail-baked bannock, soda, sourdough or fruit breads, soft tortillas.

For fillings try: cucumber, lettuce, tuna, chicken, salmon, ham flakes (mixed with celery and mayonnaise), sardines, cheese, salami, crab meat, sprouts, paté, hummus, dried beef and always peanut butter, jam and honey.

Salads are an option: early in your trip, try a Greek salad, later a cabbage, carrot and raisin and finally a three-bean (canned) salad.

Trail snacks are essential energy and pleasure givers at lunch and later when energy wanes: Gorp (a trail mix of nuts, chocolate, dried fruits), licorice, chocolate bars, granola bars, hard candies, salty peanuts and pretzels, sesame snaps, fruitcake, cookies, Baker's semi-sweet chocolate, jujubes, etc.

Try to complete the hardest part of your day before lunch. You are always at your strongest (if you have had a good breakfast) in the hours before lunch. Don't climb a mountain or attempt a lengthy portage at three o'clock.

**Dinners** On camping trips, up to eight hours a day is spent preparing and enjoying meals. The longest meal is usually dinner, the time when you can relax and enjoy the sunset and exploits of the day. If the weather is threatening, set up a good tarp-sheltered kitchen and gather enough firewood for dinner, the evening campfire and breakfast.

Serve yourself an aperitif and an appetizer to take the edge off your appetite. This will help you relax and allow the meal enough time to cook.

*Appetizer ideas* Soup, nachos and salsa, olives, sushi (try it! it's easy), vegetables and dip, bruschetta, crackers and cheese, smoked oysters, pate, hummus. Salty snacks – peanuts, goldfish, pretzels, popcorn.

*Main course ideas* These 16 meals are all made from regular, fresh or dried goods available at your grocery store. They can be cooked with just pots and fry pans.

1.   chili
2.   stir-fry chicken and vegetables
3.   lentil pilaf
4.   spaghetti and sauce
5.   curried chicken and vegetable tortillas
6.   tuna casserole
7.   beef stroganoff
8.   tacos and fresh toppings with refried beans
9.   enchiladas
10.  shepherd's pie
11.  fettucine alfredo
12.  fish chowder
13.  meat and scalloped or mashed potatoes

14. seafood casserole
15. pizza
16. quiche

## Fish feasts

It takes approximately 0.5 kg (1 lb.) of fish per person to make a main course. There are several cooking options:

- With smaller fish, fry them whole in a pan with butter and herbs.
- You can also filet your fish and fry as above.
- Sauté the flesh and add to a chowder casserole or pasta dish.
- Wrap the entire fish in tinfoil with butter, herbs, lemon and bread or vegetables and bake it on a coal for 10 minutes per pound.
- With a large fish, cut the fish through the backbone in 4 cm (1.5 in.) thick steaks and broil, fry or bake as desired.

**Dutch ovens** The Dutch oven is very old technology. It was brought over from Europe and went westward with the wagon trains. Originally made of cast iron, these ovens were too heavy for wilderness travel. But recently Dutch ovens have been successfully cast in aluminum. Although they are still not light, canoeists and rafters have adopted them whole-heartedly because of the fantastic meals they produce.

Dutch ovens come in several diameters, but the most popular set is a 30 cm (12 in.) bottom oven and a 25 cm (10 in.) top oven that nest together. The bottom pot has three legs and an inset lid with a small depression. The top oven is flat-bottomed and sits on a trivet (a tripod spacer) on top of the lid of the bottom pot when in use. Hardwood coals or charcoal briquettes are used as the heat source. Each briquette generates approximately 25°F of heat. If your recipe calls for 200°C (400°F), you would put eight burning briquettes below the base oven and six on its lid.

The trivet creates a space and a base for the smaller oven to sit on top of the lid of the bottom oven. The briquettes on the lid of the lower oven cook the top of the meal below and the bottom of the meal above. A few more briquettes on the lid of the top oven and voilà! You have two items cooking at once. Wrap both ovens in one piece of heavy-duty tinfoil to maintain maximum heat. In 30-60 minutes, you will have cooked a beautiful main course and dessert.

Dutch ovens will cook any of the previously mentioned meals better than a regular pot and fire combination. They're also good for the following specialties:

1. lasagna
2. baked beans
3. roast of beef, pork, chicken or ham
4. casseroles
5. baked potatoes and other vegetables
6. all baked breads and desserts
7. all slow-boiling meals like stew, chowder and goulash

## Dutch oven

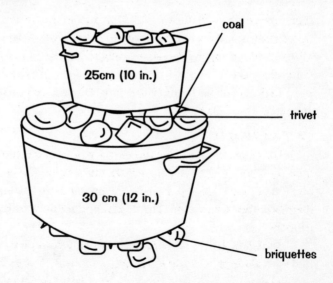

25cm (10 in.)    coal

30 cm (12 in.)    trivet

briquettes

**Desserts**  All of the following desserts can be easily prepared on the trail. Don't ignore your sweet tooth just because you're out in the wilderness!

1. no-bake cheese cake
2. Rice Krispies squares
3. date squares
4. brownies
5. rice pudding
6. Jell-O pudding
7. banana splits with whipped cream
8. Nanaimo bars
9. chocolate mousse
10. fruit with chocolate sauce
11. freeze-dried applesauce
12. fruitcakes and shortbread
13. cookies
14. doughnuts
15. peanut brittle
16. all types of cakes and pies

**Trail recipes**  There are dozens of wilderness cookbooks and specialty cookbooks to advise you on quantities and ingredients. Just remember, every time it says beat with an electric beater, you will be using a whisk and every time it says fresh milk, you will be mixing up Milko.  And if it says refrigerate overnight, you had better be camping close to a glacier.

Experiment at home with your Dutch oven – you will be amazed at your success!

## *THE WANNIGAN*

For years, the cook for the crews who worked the wilderness trails (cowboys, loggers, fishing guides, timber cruisers) used a kitchen box full of food staples, pots, pans and implements. The loggers called their box the "wannigan." This tradition continues today for canoe trippers.

Traditionalists use a varnished and reinforced plywood box carried with a tumpline (head strap) as a wannigan. New technology has produced wannigans from waterproof plastic or aluminum boxes with shoulder straps. The main idea is to create a kitchen box that has a convenient, wide opening and can be located near the fire for easy access to the contents. While you travel, the wannigan keeps everything for cooking together, organized and protected.

Backpackers and skiers have refined this concept down to a 35 x 60 cm (14 x 24 in.) cordura organizer with pockets sewn along each side to hold the implements. Most of your condiments can be purchased in small toothpaste-style tubes (mustard, mayo, horseradish) or packed in narrow- or wide-mouth Nalgene screw-top plastic containers (peanut butter, jam, butter, honey, ketchup, marmalade, oil, etc.). Dried goods (flour, salt, sugar, tea, coffee, etc.) can also be packed in Nalgene jars with refills double-bagged and packed safely at the bottom of the food barrel.

### Wannigan contents

1. a nesting set of pots suitable for the group size
2. Teflon griddle or frying pan
3. two stainless-steel mixing bowls
4. Dutch oven or gas stove
5. a fire grill, fire box or fire irons
6. pot grippers and fire gloves
7. flipper, whisk and wooden spoons
8. bread-knife, grater
9. collapsible kitchen sink and dishwashing kit
10. collapsible water jug
11. day-use staples packed in wide-mouth plastic jars
12. coffee pot
13. spice kit
14. saw (axe rarely necessary)
15. utensils (spoon, fork and knife per person)
16. nesting cup and bowl per person
17. heavy-duty tinfoil
18. matches, lighter and candle in a waterpoof container

CHAPTER FIVE

# Clothing

In the last three decades, the evolution of new fibers, fabrics and coatings has probably fuelled increased participation in outdoor recreation. Unfortunately, education in how to use this technology lags behind. The new fibers are coated to make them softer, odor-free and hydrophobic (water-repellent). They are woven to create maximum breathability, flexibility and wickability (capacity to draw water away from the skin). They can be sheared thin as underwear or left as thick fleece (100W, 200W, 300W) to serve as insulation. When combined with Lycra for stretch or shells for water- and windproof qualities, they can be effective as an outer layer.

## HOW TO DRESS FOR OUTDOOR ACTIVITIES

Hypothermia is the great enemy of outdoor enthusiasts. You lose heat through contact with cooler air, contact with circulating air (wind or motion from your activity), contact with cold liquid or solid surfaces and sometimes through accelerated loss of heat to the air through evaporation. You must control these sources of heat loss.

To do so, you need to vent heat away and manage moisture, especially during highly aerobic activities. It's not a question of stopping heat loss during these activities, more a question of matching your clothing to the level of heat and moisture your body is generating. To do this, it's best to dress in layers, use your head as a main vent and select your outer layer to allow maximum venting and moisture transfer. Let's consider four examples of dressing appropriately for different weather conditions and activities.

### Spring and fall

For spring and fall activities, you will probably want to wear a first layer of polyester underwear next to your skin. Choose under-wear that is light, fits snugly, transfers moisture rapidly and is flexible (minimum two-way stretch). You should carry in your pack a second layer – a sweater or vest or some other article of clothing. It should be polyester again, but thicker to offer insulation if the weather changes or to put on when you stop for a rest or emergency. Your outer layer should be a wind-resistant, highly breathable shell that controls heat lost due to wind or motion and protects you from abrasion.

More advanced jackets are made of an ultralight nylon with a coating or laminate that allows breathing, but prevents rain from pen-etrating the garment (just like your skin). These garments are some-what fragile because the laminate or coating can be damaged by fric-tion, salt, dirt and multiple washings. Extra venting (underarm mesh or zips, two-way zippers, flexible neck closures, back mesh vents) improves the garment's breathability and your comfort.

 Always carry a toque or hat in any season. Fifty percent of body heat is vented from the neck up. Control this primary heat vent!

### Summer

Extreme conditions can occur in the summer, especially at high-er altitudes. Fatigue, rain and cold-water sports can also lead to hypothermia, even in very warm weather. Nonetheless, your primary concerns in the summer are overheating, sunburn, insects and abra-sion. Your summer wardrobe must be as complete and flexible as your winter one. Polyester underwear and thicker, second layers are still practical. Your shirt should be loose and quick-drying with mesh underarms and back vents. The cuffs and collars should button tight against insects. Wear a wide-brim hat and use sunblock.

Modern quick-drying pants often offer a convertible option where the legs zip off turning your pants into shorts. Choose your socks carefully to offer maximum wicking of moisture away from fric-tion areas to prevent blisters. There are over 2,000 sweat glands in your feet! Choose footwear specific to your activity (like lightweight boots for day trips and heavier support boots for expedition hiking with a heavy pack).

Water sports require specific clothing for warmth and safety. Consult an expert to outfit yourself for kayaking and whitewater canoeing.

### *Winter – high aerobic activity*

Winter sports executed at a fast pace for a short time for competition or training (running, cross-country skiing, speed skating, etc.) make great demands on the athlete and clothing. Athletes should evaluate the temperature, terrain, wind chill and how they feel before choosing the level of insulation to match the body's ability to generate enough heat to stay comfortable during the exercise. This means they will vary the weight of the first layer of polyester underwear next to their skin and the outer layer of Lycra/polyester that forms their tights and top. Extra protection is required for the ears (light earmuffs, headband or balaclava), face (face mask on cold days to warm the air before it is breathed in, and to protect the neck, cheeks and nose), groin (men's polyester briefs should have a front wind panel) and chest (women's polyester sports bras offer support and protection). Athletes will often do warm-ups in an additional outer layer – a vest or breathable windshell that will be put aside when the workout begins or carried in a pack for rest stops.

In winter athletes must remember they are losing a great deal of energy and moisture. They must drink constantly and carry an energy food source. Frostnip occurs frequently in athletes who do not dress and drink properly. Heat the air you breathe through a scarf or face mask on extremely cold days.

### *Winter touring and leisure activities*

If your winter touring activities are very sedentary (walking the dog, snowmobiling, spectator sports) you should dress in layers with the first layer considerably thicker than aerobic underwear and the last layer an insulated parka (either down or fiberfill). Protect your feet with good socks and insulated boots. Remember mitts are warmer than gloves and a good hat and scarf will control that main heat loss area, your head.

Most winter touring activities are self-propelled, with lots of stops and starts. You'll find yourself sitting outdoors, or moving at a slow pace in activities such as ski touring, snowshoeing, winter camping, nature walks, alpine skiing, snowboarding and leisure skating. To stay warm – but not too warm – your wardrobe needs a first layer that is light, a second layer that will vary from a 100-300 gram weight of fleece (depending on the temperature) and an outer shell of a heavier, tougher fabric with pockets and venting. Winter-touring participants must concentrate on accessories that will extend the stay outdoors: hat, mitts, gloves, face mask, chemical heat packs, sunglasses, sunblock, matches, water bottle, extra socks and energy bars should all be carried in a comfortable fanny or day pack.

The 10 features of a good touring winter shell include:

1. a tough outer fiber of windproof but breathable material
2. this outer fiber is laminated to a membrane or coating that makes the fiber waterproof yet breathable – this treatment should be inside and protected with a lining
3. bright colors, for safety
4. big zippers (#8 or 10) with pull tabs and Velcro closures, friendly to mitt-clad hands
5. all seams welded shut with breathable tape
6. roomy enough to accommodate three internal layers
7. drawstrings at the hip and waist to act as snow-powder cuffs and trap warm air
8. underarm venting zippers, pockets that vent and two-way front zippers as temperature control features
9. a well-designed hood (moves with your head, stiff peak, interior and exterior adjustments, tucks away or lies flat). Expedition parkas do not have removable hoods for safety but recreational parkas do offer this as an option.
10. Closures over all vents! For extreme conditions, your front zip, pockets, neck, cuffs, waist and hip closures must all be covered or otherwise capable of completely sealing in warmth.

## *EMERGENCY CLOTHING*

In an emergency situation, remember:

- Seek shelter from wind, rain and snow.
- Put or wrap something on your head and neck.
- Use whatever is available for an outer shell; wrap yourself in a tarp, blanket, plastic, garbage bag, pieces of birchbark.
- Stuff your clothing with anything dry as an insulating layer to trap air (crumpled up sections of newspaper, cattails, bunches of dried grass, leaves, foam).
- Tighten down all cuffs and collars to trap air.
- Sit on something dry – foam, cardboard, wood – to insulate your body from the ground. Or keep moving, pacing and circulating arms at a pace just fast enough to keep warm until help arrives.

# CHAPTER SIX

# Wings, fangs, claws and poison

In Canada, we are fortunate: our climate and cold winters do not appeal to many poisonous or predatory species of wildlife or even plants. But common-sense precautions can go a long way to protecting you from discomfort due to animal bites or allergic reactions. Let's begin with two basic rules on dealing with your natural neighbors.

**First rule:** Any mammal, fish, reptile, or insect that is frightened, trapped, feeding or protecting its young (or its home) will fight back with startling speed and ferocity.

**Second rule:** *Any* species that is wounded or sick or behaving abnormally should be avoided at all costs! Rabies is a dangerous disease transmitted through the saliva of infected animals. Foxes, raccoons, skunks, coyotes, cats, dogs and squirrels are notorious carriers.

Develop habits when travelling through wildlands that are cautious and defensive.

For safe travel, teach yourself to identify:

- poison ivy
- bear tracks and scat
- hornet and bee nests
- rattlesnakes
- animal dens
- animal trails, scat and kills

A good plant, animal, bird and reptile identification field book (like the Peterson or Audubon guides) is a great companion on a trip. Carry it with you until identification of the list above becomes second-nature.

## Teach your children these nine common-sense rules:

1. Always keep a clean campsite.
2. Do not keep any food (even toothpaste) close to or in your tent.
3. Do not camp on animal trails, near dens or feeding grounds or at any site that is dirty or near a dump.
4. Do not reach into a firepit to rearrange stones without checking for snakes or nests.
5. Do not reach into any log or hole without checking for tenants.
6. Do not sit on a log, stump or rock without checking for ants, hornets, ticks, etc.
7. Do not remove a fishhook with your bare hands from deep in a fish's mouth.
8. Do not handle dead animals with your bare hands.
9. Do not feed or tease wildlife.

Here's a selection of the various dangerous animals and plants you'll encounter in the wildlands of Canada – with a few notes on how to deal with them.

### REPTILES

Canada has two species of poisonous snakes: the small and rare massassauga rattlesnake found in the Georgian Bay area and the large prairie rattlesnake found in our grasslands. Rattlesnakes can be recognized by their diamond-shaped heads and warning rattle (the sound made by dry skin inside the end of their tail). Snakes will usually coil and warn before striking and will seek an escape route if allowed.

*Treatment* Although painful (burning pain, swelling, numbness) Canadian snake bites are rarely fatal.

- Try to slow the circulation of venom-tainted blood to the heart.
- Wipe, wash and disinfect the wound.
- Calm the victim to reduce the heartbeat.
- Evacuate to a doctor for an anti-venom injection.
- Otherwise treat for swelling and shock.
- Tourniquets or compress bandages will slow down circulation and help slow release of the poison. Remember, tourniquets must be released slowly every 20-30 minutes.
- Professional equipment for a first-aid kit for trips in poisonous-snake territory should include an extractor with suction cups.
- **Do not** try to extract venom by cutting and sucking the wound – this only works in Hollywood westerns.

## *INSECTS*

It is common for individuals exposed for the first time to bites from blackflies, mosquitoes and other biting insects to have a mild allergic reaction. Some people seem more conditioned or immune to insects; others will experience swelling, itching and some pain.

*Treatment* Cold compresses, bathing with a saline solution or antihistamines will relieve insect bites.

Use of insect repellents with high concentrations of DEET, clothing with tight closings and DEET-impregnated mesh (bug jackets and pants) is a wise precaution for northern travel. Insect bites and the constant annoyance of buzzing insects can wear down an individual's tolerance. In a survival situation, this can contribute significantly to a lack of energy and willpower. This is a great danger and should not be underestimated. Mud can serve as a protective layer in an emergency.

**Bees and hornets** It is very important that you know ahead of time just how you react to a bee or hornet sting. Reactions will range from mild pain, to hives, to anaphylactic shock that can result in death. If you have a history of severe reactions to stings, *always* inform your travelling partners and carry an injectable self-administered epinephrine kit. Allergic reactions are nearly immediate and the injection should be given within 1-2 minutes of the sting.

**Spiders, ants, ticks, leeches**  Some Canadian spiders and ants can give a painful bite that may swell, but there are no known poisonous species (unless they arrive with a load of imported produce).

Ticks and leeches attach themselves to the skin and – through a painless bite – begin feeding on our blood. Leeches may be removed with coaxing or salt and are little danger.

Ticks are not yet common in Canada, but they are a serious problem in the northeastern United States. Lyme disease is one of several unpleasant diseases transmitted by ticks. Hikers and canoeists in the Appalachians, Minnesota and all the northeastern parks should:

- Check themselves and their partners for ticks at each rest stop (look especially at your neck, legs, hair).
- Use insect repellent on themselves and a spray on their equipment.
- Wear protective clothing.
- Remove ticks slowly, allowing them to release rather than leave saliva (or their head) in the bite.
- If the bite produces redness and swelling, see a doctor.

## POISONOUS PLANTS

There are several species of plants whose needles, nettles and thorns will scratch and spear you, but only three species will create an allergic reaction externally: poison ivy, poison oak and poison sumac.

**Poison ivy** is the most common. This three-leafed ground cover or vine, when touched, leaves a resin on the skin and clothing that can be spread by touching other skin.  If you accidentally touch poison ivy, your skin and clothing should be washed immediately with soap and water.  If a rash occurs, oral antihistamines (from your first-aid kit), cool compresses or mud will help relieve the itch.

**Poison oak** and **poison sumac** (not the common red sumac) are rare in Canada. Poison oak is common in the western United States and poison sumac in the south and in small pockets of southern Ontario and Quebec.  Treat in a similar way to poison ivy.

## CARNIVORES

The large carnivores, bears, wolves, cougars and wolverines, are definitely a source of childhood nightmares, but in reality these large animals are the true marks of a healthy wilderness. These beautiful creatures require huge tracts of wilderness to hunt, breed and flourish. A decline in their population is a key early warning that we are not protecting the wilderness ecosystem.

Although any of these large animals has the capability of hunting and killing humans, they almost never do. For the most part, they view man as a natural enemy, to be avoided at all costs. It is true that these animals, if trapped, wounded, teased or surprised will attack to protect their young or their food. In some cases, an old animal, no longer capable of hunting, will begin to eat garbage and become dangerous. More often, bears (especially) will become used to acquiring an easy meal from campers' packs and kitchens. These bears are dangerous because they may become bold and confrontational if challenged. There is a very small percentage of bears and cougars that are predatory.

### First aid

*Any scratch or bite from domestic or wild animals has great potential to become infected.* Wash it thoroughly with soap and water and a stronger disinfectant, if possible, or saline water. Cover the wound with a sterile dressing and wrap (not tape) the gauze in place. See a doctor immediately, otherwise treat for infection (see Chapter 2 on first-aid). Do not handle the animal or reptile if it has been killed or captured. Transport it in a cage or bag for rabies testing. If this is not practical, a sample of the brain tissue can be tested.

Bears have poor eyesight, but a keen sense of smell and hearing. Your first line of defense travelling through bear country is to make your presence *known* (ring a bear bell, whistle, or sing as you hike) and keep your campsite *unknown* (keep a clean campsite, clean your fish well away from camp, hang or seal your food in air-tight containers).

Your second line of defense is to watch for bear signs – tracks, torn-up logs and earth, scat, fresh kills – and avoid areas where a bear may be hunting or sleeping. If you see signs of a bear, avoid dense foliage where you may surprise the bear.

Your third line of defense is if you do see a bear is three-fold:

- Make noise.
- Move downwind.
- Allow the bear to identify you and retreat.

The three lines of defense, above, should help you avoid dealing with bears at close range. But if your encounter with a bear is close, immediate and aggressive, you'll need to take other steps:

- Stop; step back slowly.
- Speak calmly (this will also help you calm down, too).
- Adopt a relaxed, non-threatening posture.

Carefully retreat! If the bear decides to attack, you'll face a diffi-cult set of choices. For black bears, it's best to fight back with any weapon you have. Pepper spray works at close range (3-5 m from an upwind position); so does a real gun of sufficient caliber. Grizzly bears, however, will sometimes leave you alone if you "play dead."

If you are going to camp in bear country on a regular basis, learn to use the pepper-spray gun or a real gun for your own protection.

# CHAPTER SEVEN

# Weather, navigation and self-rescue

Because staying put is your best option for being rescued, any decision to move must have these prerequisites. Ask yourself:

1. Is this really going to improve my options or am I just bored? (If you can't answer yes, wait another two days.)
2. Do I really have the strength and clothing to walk over rough terrain? (If the answer is no, save your strength for gathering food and water close to your base.)
3. Do I really have any idea where I am or where I'm going? (If the answer is no, don't risk increasing the severity of your situation.)
4. Do I have food and shelter to carry with me? (If the answer is no, over 50 percent of your travel time will be required for these two activities.)
5. If you are part of a group, is the group's position improved or weakened by your attempt to go for help? (Bravado does not assist survival; leadership decisions do.)

When you are convinced moving to improve your position, food supply or chance of rescue is the right choice, then do so with caution and with a plan. Travelling through wilderness terrain takes a lot of energy, something that may be in short supply.

### BEFORE YOU LEAVE
- Make a plan. Where is help? Use reasonable assumptions about the geography, identifiable landmarks, cardinal directions and probable distance.
- Draw a map. Illustrate your thoughts and add in any visual

landmarks you can see from a higher point. Mark in the cardinal directions confirmed by your compass, the North Star and sun.

- Do an inventory and prepare. Take all the useful tools, food and water you can comfortably carry. Repair your clothing.
- Leave a message. Use ground-to-air code (see chart on page 64) and a written message with anyone you are leaving behind.
- Plan a signal. If the opportunity to signal for help arrives as you travel, how will you do it (whistle, mirror, smoke, three of anything)?
- Travel with a partner if possible.

## WHILE TRAVELLING

Follow your plan. Move from landmark to landmark in one cardinal direction; downstream is a logical choice. Expand your map along the way. Add in more information as you make visual contact.

Go slowly. Use natural trails that go in your general direction (game trails, water courses). Don't fight the natural situation. Go around hills, swamps, lakes – not over or through them. Don't cross large bodies of water. Cold water and wet clothes are an added danger.

Stay in more open areas where there is easier walking, fewer bugs and a breeze. In such locations it is easier to see and be seen unless the weather is really foul. Ridge lines may be your best route during the day if the walking is not to difficult.

Stop early and stop often to rest, gather food and water and re-evaluate. If you find a great shelter, take a day off to regain your strength and repair your kit. Don't travel in bad weather unless you absolutely have to. Along the way, follow the example of Hansel in the fairy tale – leave signs and messages regarding your direction of travel and time.

## FINDING NORTH: FOUR TECHNIQUES

**Compass** The dark (usually red) end of the needle in your compass will point to the magnetic north pole (360˚). True north is either east (least) or west (best) of magnetic north. True north runs along a line in Canada connecting Thunder Bay, Churchill and the North Pole. If you are west of true north you will have to add the compass bearing to find a true direction of travel; if you are east of this line you will have to subtract the compass bearing. (If you have a topographic map it will tell you the +/- declination in the margin. Otherwise for travel in an emergency situation, just use the compass as a general reference.)

When you face north where the needle is pointed, east is 90° to your right, west 90° to your left, south directly behind you (180°). Draw this on your survival map with some visual landmarks (mountain is north, lake is south, pine ridge is east and the big tree is west). Keep building your map as you advance from major landmark to landmark. Not adjusting for a 10° declination will put you off-course approximately 88 feet per mile. (Newfoundland has a declination of approximately 25°W and Victoria 25°E.)

**North Star** In Canada, the North Star is our guiding light. On a clear night, the big dipper is a very dominant constellation. The two outside stars (not top, not bottom, not inside) of the bucket portion of the dipper point toward the North Star (Polaris). When you are facing the North Star, you are facing north. Draw an arrow in the ground, but save any travel for daylight.

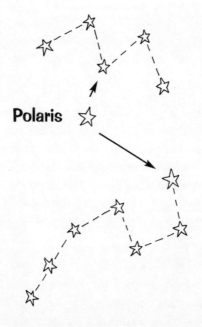

**Sundial compass** The sun moves east to west over the course of a day. A 60 cm (24 in.) stick staked straight 90° into the ground in the morning will cast a shadow. By marking the progression of the shadow on an hourly basis, you can determine the cardinal points. Mark the end of the shadow each hour. The shortest shadow will be at noon, the longest in the morning pointing west, and evening pointing east. North and south will be on your right (S) and left (N) as you face east.

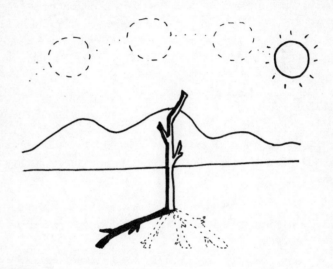

**Watch compass** At 6 a.m. the sun rises in the east, at noon it is due south and 6 p.m. it is due west.

1. Place a match size stick in a circle of flat ground you've swept clean.
2. Lay your watch beside the stick with the shadow of the stick falling directly across the hour hand.
3. Divide the angle between the hour hand and 12 in half and draw a line across the face and onto the ground. This line will point south as long as it is before 6 p.m. (North is opposite, east is left and west is right.)

# Determining sunset

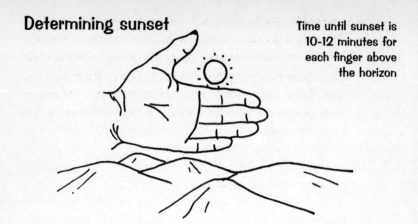

Time until sunset is **10-12 minutes** for each finger above the horizon

## WEATHER

Your base camp and self-rescue travel zone will have their own microclimate. Here are some general observations you can make at home that might make you more comfortable and successful in a rescue situation.

- The south- and west-facing shoreline or hillsides tend to get the most daylight and heat; therefore they are dryer and warmer.
- Conversely, the north and east will be cooler during the day, but damp for sleeping or collecting wood.
- Breezes generally travel from cool areas to warm ones because warm air rapidly rises and expands and the heavier cool air moves to fill the void. Midday, when the land is hot and the water cooler, air will move on-shore. At night, when the land cools faster than the water, the reverse happens – an off-shore breeze.
- A climb of 300 m (1,000 ft.) of elevation will cool the air (and you) by 3°C.
- A 10 km/hr (6 mile/hour) wind will "chill" your exposed skin by 5°C.
- If there is some humidity in the air (no moisture = 0 percent humidity and precipitation = 100 percent humidity), dew, mist or fog will occur when the humid air is warmer than

the earth. The greater the humidity, the thicker the fog.

- Precipitation occurs when the humidity reaches the saturation point (100 percent) in the clouds. A cloud is really only suspended moisture or ice droplets awaiting the "trigger." Think of a cloud as a floating sponge. The hot-air sponge is bigger than the cold-air sponge but the amount of moisture remains the same. The smaller (cold) sponge cannot hold the same amount of moisture as the big (warm) sponge. The colder it gets, the more the atmosphere squeezes that humidity and eventually it falls as rain, ice or another unpleasant combination. Air cooling occurs violently (vertical currents) or gradually over hundreds of miles as a warm front overtakes (it is expanding and rising) the slower cold front. The prevailing winds are moving both fronts in the same direction.

- White puffy vertical clouds, when they build vertically and form a black anvil top are violent thunderstorm clouds known as **cumulonimbus**. Take cover – a short violent lightning-filled rain or hail storm is on the way. The moisture inside the cloud travels on air currents to heights of 9,000 m/30,000 ft. (ask pilots) and cools so rapidly that the droplets become saturated quickly at a temperature that forms ice. When it doesn't melt on the way down, it comes down as hail.

## PREDICTING WEATHER
### Signs of rainy weather
1. Clear skies begin to show wispy clouds (cirrus clouds).
2. Thicker layering occurs at high levels (stratus clouds) – perhaps you noticed no stars and a warmer night.
3. Clouds drop lower and thicken – perhaps the sunrise was red through these clouds.
4. Wind direction changes as the low-pressure, ground-level winds from the south and east make the leaves turn upside down.
5. Finally rain starts slowly. Do you have enough firewood for 36 hours? If there is not a good wind blowing, a solid rain could last that long.

# Side view of warm front with clouds and rain

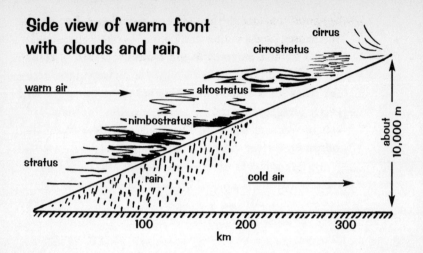

warm air

cirrus

cirrostratus

altostratus

nimbostratus

stratus

rain

cold air

about 10,000 m

100    200    300

km

# Side view of cold front

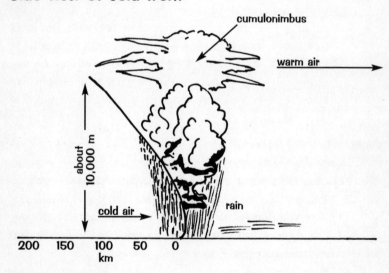

cumulonimbus

warm air

about 10,000 m

cold air

rain

200   150   100   50   0

km

*Signs of good weather*

1. Red sunset, bright moon.
2. Clouds forming in vertical pillows rather than horizontal layers.
3. The wind shifts to blow from the northwest or west.
4. The fog burns off quickly.
5. Your boots are dry and your fire is still burning in the morning.

## EMERGENCY SIGNALS

If you have made an emergency landing in a plane or helicopter, an emergency locator beacon should already be signalling your position to a series of satellites circling the earth. They will triangulate your position and relay that information to the rescue technicians. Similarly you can carry an EPIRB (emergency position indicator radio beacon) which you can set off to trigger the same response. (This is a serious matter and it must be a life-threatening emergency. Don't call for help because a bear ate your food or you got wet in the rain.)

There are now satellite phones that are portable enough for use anywhere. These work off solar or lithium batteries to allow them to be taken on extreme wilderness expeditions. Although they communicate via satellites, they work just like a phone and do not trigger an emergency response team unless requested.

Global Positioning System (GPS) navigational aids are also wonderful navigational tools that work by collecting radio signals transmitted by GPS satellites and triangulating your position on the ground. However, GPS is not a communication device, only a navigational aid. Any GPS system is only as good as its batteries and your knowledge of how to use it.

The Transport Canada signals on the next page are to be used to communicate with aircraft when an emergency exists. Symbols 1 to 5 are internationally accepted; 6 to 9 are for use in Canada only.

| Number | Message | Code symbol |
|--------|---------|-------------|
| 1 | require assistance | V |
| 2 | require medical assistance | X |
| 3 | no (or negative) | N |
| 4 | yes (or affirmative) | Y |
| 5 | proceeding this direction | → |
| 6 | all is well | L L |
| 7 | require food and water | F |
| 8 | require fuel and oil | L |
| 9 | need repairs | W |

Transport Canada advises that you should use strips of fabric or parachute, pieces of wood, stones or any other available material to make the symbols. Your goal should be to provide as much of a color contrast as possible between the material used for the symbols and the background against which the symbols are exposed.

Symbols should be at least 2.4 m (8 ft.) in height or larger, if possible. Care should be taken to lay out symbols exactly as depicted to avoid confusion with other symbols. A space of 3 m (10 ft.) should separate the elements of symbol 6.

Three of anything (fires, people, canoes, signal tarps) arranged in a large triangle, placed a minimum of 3 m (10 ft.) apart, is the universal signal for help.

CHAPTER EIGHT

# Leadership and group behavior

Leadership is both a learned skill and a thinking process. It is a natural combination of calmness under pressure and confidence in one's ability to handle a situation. Today, there are community colleges, universities and traditional wilderness leadership schools, like N.O.L.E.S. (National Outdoor Leadership and Education School) and Outward Bound, that offer four-week to four-year courses on how to become a professional outdoor leader. While no course can guarantee calm under pressure, training in wilderness lore certainly boosts a person's confidence.

Each outdoor discipline – skiiing, climbing, kayaking, canoeing, rafting, sailing, winter travel, etc. – has its own set of educational opportunities and certification measurements. Whitewater-canoeing guides, for example, would have the following skills on their résumé:

- CPR certification
- wilderness first-aid technician certification
- Canadian Canoe Association level-three whitewater instructor
- swift-water rescue technician certification
- Bronze swimming medallion
- basic sensitivity and psychology of behavior training
- a list of routes they have guided or travelled as part of a group

The best companies still apprentice new guides with experienced guides to evaluate the intangibles before putting them in a position of total responsibility for a group of wilderness campers. The intangibles include:

- sense of humor
- sensitivity to the needs of others
- motivation of self and others
- endurance
- moral ethics
- personality under pressure
- patience

In a crisis situation, a leader is not necessarily the strongest, loudest or best-educated member of the party. A group should select an individual who is calm, logical and internally strong. This person can probably control and motivate the group into cohesive action using everyone's specific strengths for specific tasks.

If you are assigned or assume the role of leadership, then you are taking these responsibilities:

1. You will evaluate your group's skills, strengths and weaknesses (do not plan a trip or a challenge that exceeds the group's abilities).
2. You will evaluate your own skills and experience honestly (don't take responsibility or make decisions that exceed your personal skill level).
3. You will endeavor to raise the skill level of the group by teaching them the skills they will need.
4. You will also teach them respect for the land, natural laws and the individuals in the group.
5. You will not put your personal goals before the needs of the group (but you must look after your own health and safety for the good of everyone).
6. You will strive to be sensitive to the psychological needs of the group (physical first aid to an injured person is obvious; psychological first aid to a person in fear, denial or with poor social skills is much more difficult).

Leadership-training courses teach leaders to prevent crises by planning ahead and being prepared. To do this, you need route knowledge, weather knowledge, knowledge of the group's limitations and a contingency plan.

**Route knowledge** Route knowledge is everything you can learn about your route that will help you plan the timing of your trip. It includes whatever you know or can learn about distance, terrain, elevation, hazards, distractions, water supply, water levels, snow conditions, roads and communication points. By allowing the right amount of time, you will avoid a crisis caused by hurrying or waiting. You will also bring the right equipment.

**Weather knowledge** Hypothermia and dehydration can happen anywhere, any season. By knowing the extremes in the weather for your trip, you can pack the proper personal clothing and menu. That will help get you and your group ready for difficulties, should they arise.

**Group knowledge** Knowing the personal skills and limitations of each member of your group will assist you in assigning tasks and loads, planning the pace of the trip and allowing each individual to contribute to the group. Knowing medical histories and past performance on other trips will forewarn you of possible problems.

**Contingency Plan** Good leaders believe in Murphy's Law: If something can go wrong, it will. On a wilderness expedition, something will certainly go wrong despite the best planning. If you are lucky, it will be a minor cut, a broken pole or a raccoon in the supplies. If you are unlucky, it could be a lost person, a grizzly encounter or a medical emergency. Your contingency plan is the essential ace up your sleeve.

In a crisis, remember that first aid is always the *second* priority. First, organize the group so that no further damage is done and then go into action. Your route knowledge will allow you to make the right decision to communicate with outside help. Lucky leaders are most often the ones who plan properly and proceed logically; unlucky ones take short cuts.

## PARTICIPATING IN A COMMERCIAL OR PRIVATE EXPEDITION

There are many different kinds of expeditions for today's adventure traveller. On the one hand, you might pay a professional outfitter to organize all the logistics, equipment, food and finances as well as find other like-minded individuals for a trip. On the other, you might be part of a group of friends inexperienced in the wilderness but gung-ho to do it on your own. In either case, before you sign on, you must realize your personal responsibilities:

1.  You must acknowledge that a wilderness expedition has some element of risk. There are always uncontrollable circumstances. You must be willing to accept the uncertainties and the consequences that may follow from them (commercial companies will ask you to sign a waiver to this effect).

2.  You must be ready to prepare yourself physically and mentally for the challenges of the trip. Wilderness travel is usually not too demanding when done at the right pace, but portaging, hiking or skiing with 23 kg (50 lbs.) on your back will place a higher demand on your body and your mind than you may be used to.

3.  You must equip yourself properly for the challenges of the route and climate. If you don't have a warm sleeping bag and insulating pad, you won't have a good night's sleep in most of Canada's wilderness. If you are unprotected from rain, sun, cold or bugs, you are risking your personal safety at the expense of the group. This is unacceptable.

4.  You must agree to follow the leadership decisions of the group. Your individual freedom to make decisions must be sacrificed as part of the group. The group must move as one, act safely as one and protect and support each other. A wilderness situation gives you neither the time nor the environment for participatory democracy.

5.  You must be willing to conduct yourself with social grace within the norms and ethics of the group (if a commercial expedition, within the ethics of the company). This could involve environmental practices, hygiene practices, socially acceptable behavior and simply striving to get along.

On a wilderness journey, you sleep alone or with a partner, you ski or hike at your own pace, essentially alone, you canoe with a partner and (except at mealtimes) you are not required to interact a great deal with the group. However, most wilderness trips are a great bonding experience. They can lead to lifelong friendships as you and those in your group learn to deal with the natural environment.

CHAPTER NINE

# Wilderness connoisseur

In the first chapter, we used the dictionary definition of wilderness as "inhospitable, uninhabitable, barren." It would be incorrect to leave you with this impression of wilderness. The wilderness today is becoming increasingly valuable due to its rarity. The late naturalist-filmmaker Bill Mason, one of Canada's greatest voices for wilderness preservation, created this image of the environment for us:

"Wilderness is like icebergs drifting in a sea. Everything man does in the name of development increases the temperature of the water and therefore the rate at which wilderness disappears."

The world was wilderness before humans arrived and will retreat back to wilderness when we are gone. For many years, there were so few humans and so much wilderness that we threatened only a small portion of the planet. That has changed as wilderness areas have become increasingly threatened by civilization.

It is important, then, for anyone travelling in the wild to become a wilderness connoisseur. In this way, you can enjoy the wonderful wilderness experiences remaining in the world and speak passionately for the preservation of our remaining natural environments.

A wilderness experience is a combination of:

- the natural environment
- the stimulation you receive from it
- the makeup of the group you choose to travel with
- your method of travel

Canadians choose most often to travel in small groups, *softly* through the wilderness by foot, canoe, kayak, skis, snowshoes, mountain bikes, horses and rafts. Others choose to visit the edge of the wilderness by cruise ship, camper or wilderness lodge. Others visit the wilderness vicariously through films, books and paintings.

The "wilderness icebergs" remaining in Canada are often found within our parks in the south and, to some extent, throughout Crown land in the north. Our national and provincial parks systems are built on a wilderness connoisseur premise. Geographers divide Canada into 39 regions and several more significantly unique divisions within each region. Each natural region is significantly different in terms of vegetation, wildlife and terrain. For example, you would have a much different experience hiking B.C.'s West Coast Rainforest Trail than you would hiking the Skyline Ridge Trail in the Rockies. Your wild-river canoe trip down one of the whitewater mountain rivers running out of the Mackenzie Mountains would be much different from a trip through the mixed forests, lakes and waterways of Algonquin Park.

Each region offers you opportunities to experience a different type of wilderness. And each season changes the wilderness experience again. Algonquin is very different in the dead of winter on snowshoes than it is in the peak of the summer canoe season.

Our parks systems have been selected to conserve the best representative samples of each natural region. Unfortunately, political objectives don't always coincide with best conservation practices. Some commercial activities and forms of advertising designed to attract visitors may not always coincide with a wilderness connoisseur's ideal experience. You may be wise to adjust your trip's timing to the off-season in the busier parks, or spend a little more money to pay for air access to the interior.

Conservation groups closely watch the conflicts between political interests and good conservation practices. Their common goal is to see 12 percent of Canada's wild landscapes in legally protected areas. Currently only seven percent is protected (only three percent when you exclude those areas where logging, mining and hunting are allowed).

Currently some of the world's greatest wilderness exists in Canada's North. A trip by canoe across the barren lands, by ski or dog team to the North Pole, or by foot into the wildest mountains of the Mackenzie range or Ellesmere and Baffin islands are considered among the most exotic wilderness trips in the world.

But a wilderness experience doesn't have to be to remote areas or into difficult environments to provide a wonderful experience for a wilderness connoisseur. Today's equipment, navigational aids, trail food, outdoor clothing and professional outfitters make any trip you may dream of a real option for you. You and your group of travelling companions can acquire the skills and equipment to begin a lifelong collection of wilderness experiences. You might also choose never to visit the extremes of wilderness, yet work to preserve their character by your donations and spoken word. You don't have to see and touch Michelangelo's David to know it is a rare masterpiece. Similarly, you don't have to set foot in the Arctic to realize that this unique environment deserves our protection and appreciation.

It is not a tendency of governments to give first priority to conservation. Remember, wilderness is still a location of confusion: uncharted, unplanned, uncontrolled and untapped space for most of the general public. Most voters want jobs, electric power, minerals, water, lumber and wealth rather than a wilderness they may never visit or understand. Wilderness preservation just doesn't sell as a vote-getting plank in a politician's election strategy. How then do those of us who believe in the value of wilderness speak out for its preservation?

## WILDERNESS PRESERVATION GROUPS

Some groups – like Ducks Unlimited, Trout Unlimited, Federation of Ontario Naturalists, Atlantic Salmon Federation, Ruffed Grouse Society, Canadian Wildlife Federation and many others – focus on wildlife species and their habitat to measure the health of a wildland's ecosystem. If we can preserve the most-fragile inhabitants, they reason, then we protect the rest of the ecosystem. It is much easier to focus the public's attention on one element of a problem than the complex issues of environmental preservation.

Other groups are associated with a particular watershed, park or landscape for the same reason: Temagami Wilderness Society, Valhalla Wilderness Society, Western Canada Wilderness Committee, Friends of Algonquin, Friends of the Stikine, Island Nature Trust, Alberta Wilderness Association and many others. Their watchdog presence really helps protect local areas.

A few trust funds and conservation groups put all their resources into buying title to the land or waterscape in danger. This way there is no more debate about the land's future – it is conserved forever. The Nature Conservancy of Canada (110 Eglinton Ave. W., Suite 400, Toronto, Ontario M4R 1A3) is probably the most successful organization of this nature.

Other organizations put their trust in the law and retain legal counsel to challenge infractions to environmental-protection laws. The Sierra Legal Defense Fund and the Canadian Environmental Law Group are two of the most successful legal guardian angels.

Finally, the national organizations that lobby on our behalf and speak out for stronger conservation and environmental-protection government policies need our support:

- The Canadian Nature Federation, 1 Nicholas St., Site 606, Ottawa, Ontario K1N 7B7 represents over 100 naturalist groups in Canada.
- The Canadian Parks and wilderness Society, 401 Richmond St. W., Site 380, Toronto, Ontario M5V 3A8 has chapters in each region speaking out for better management of existing parks and conservation of more wilderness areas.
- The Canadian Arctic Resources Committee, 7 Hinton Ave. N., Suite 200, Ottawa, Ontario K1Y 4P1 is a strong voice for logical management of all resources including wilderness in the Arctic.
- The World Wildlife Fund, 245 Eglinton Ave. E., Suite 410, Toronto, Ontario M4P 3J1 leads the campaign to protect endangered species by protecting their habitat.
- The Sierra Club of Canada, 1 Nicholas St., Suite 620, Ottawa, Ontario K1N 7B7 is an eloquent spokesperson for good environmental policies in Canada, as its counterpart is in the United States.
- The Canadian Wildlife Federation, 2740 Queensview Drive, Ottawa, Ontario K2B 1A2 represents wildlife conservation for anglers and hunters.
- Wildlife Habitat Canada, 7 Hinton Ave. N., Ottawa, Ontario K1Y 4P1 focuses on private and public land policies that maintain and enhance wildlife habitats.

- The Assembly of First Nations, 1 Nicholas St., Ottawa, Ontario K1N 7B7 has a great stake in the wilderness since a large percentage of wildlands remain under First Nations treaty rights.

Any one of these national organizations can put you in touch with a local conservation group that matches your personal style and philosophy. The bottom line is simple: Nothing is free. If you believe in wilderness as an important component of the Canadian landscape, you are going to have to stand up and say so with your voice and your wallet. Make a donation to one or more of these groups annually (it's tax-deductible) and let our politicians know where you stand.

# Glossary

As manufacturers compete for a share of the rapidly expanding market of outdoor clothing and equipment, new products emerge to confuse both the novice and the wilderness connoisseur. This glossary may assist you in product selection.

**1000 D Cordura** The original 1000 denier yarn-fiber material is the standard for toughness and abrasion resistance in the outdoor industry. It is used mostly in packs, footwear and other high-abrasion points. (The D stands for denier, a measurement for the mass in grams of textile yarns.)

**Cordura Plus** A lighter, softer version of the original, which can be blended with other fibers for softness, stretch or texture. Good for clothing or less-stressed areas (500 D Cordura, 300 D, 160 D, plus natural).

**Ballistic cloth** A very heavy, very tough denier nylon used to withstand extreme abrasion and tearing (used in bullet proof vests).

**Closed-cell foam** Foam can come in the form of a sponge that absorbs air or water, or in the form of a closed cell, a harder foam with air pockets sealed off. This airolite or ensolite foam makes an excellent insulating pad for sitting or sleeping or padding backpacks.

**Cotton** This natural fiber is still the most comfortable, cool material for clothing. Although it will absorb 40 percent of its weight in moisture, this has a cooling effect when that moisture evaporates. Canvas is a heavy form of cotton.

**DEET** The most powerful insect repellent additive known. Very hard on sensitive skin. Will melt plastic.

**DWR** Durable Water Repellent (DWR) is a treatment put on the face of garment fabrics to repel water (but it can wear away with washings).

**Goose-down fill** The best down is from Europe and is graded according to its ability to "loft" and thereby fill space. A measurement of 600+ inches filled by one ounce of down is good; 750 is excellent. Down is still considered the warmest fill per ounce (when dry).

**Gore-Tex** World's first waterproof, windproof, breathable fabric. Gore-Tex is actually a membrane with nine-million pores per square inch, each of which is 20,000 times smaller than a water droplet but 700 times larger than a water-vapor molecule. Liquid will not penetrate but perspiration can escape at a certain rate. (Gore-Tex is a registered trademark, but materials from other manufacturers try to achieve similar results.)

**2-ply/3-ply** This Gore-Tex membrane is laminated to two or three layers of fabric. Depending on its desired use, the garment manufacturer will choose a light 2-ply combination or a tougher 3-ply layup.

**Hollofil, Quallofil, Dacron II, Thinsulate, Lite Loft, Primaloft, Microloft (and others)** This group of trademarked fiberfills permits manufacturers to choose from a wide variety of insulations for garments and sleeping bags. Because of varying licensing fees, costs are not always related to quality. Observe what the brand-name leaders (North Face, Sierra Designs, Marmot Designs, Mountain Equipment Co-op) are using as a fill – it is safe to assume that it currently performs at the highest standard for an artificial fill.

**Nextec Epic** This process encapsulates individual fibers before they are woven into yards of material. Epic is windproof and water-repellent and appears to be the next generation of DWR superiority.

**PCR fleece** Post-consumer recycled fleece is made from recycled plastic bottles that are washed, ground up, melted then extruded as a fine fiber. These fibers are combined with virgin polyester to produce fleece yard goods that are cut and sewn into garments. This helps save air quality, oil, energy, water and landfill space, yet still produces a beautiful product.

**PSI** Pounds per square inch is a military measurement of water-proofness. A Gore-Tex jacket is said to have an 80 PSI waterproof measurement. The floor of a North Face expedition tent is built with 165 PSI nylon. The tent PSI is created with five layers of polyurethane coating.

**Polarguard fill** Three generations of Polarguard – classic, HV and 3D – reflect the evolution of this continuous-filament polyester fiber. This fiber continues to evolve to be softer and to have more loft, trapping air in three dimensions: inside itself, outside itself and between the filaments. This allows for a non-water-absorbent fiber to be used as a fill in garments and sleeping bags.

**Polartec** The trademark name of the leading manufacturer (Malden Mills) of a group of weights of fleece (Polartec 100/200/300). Polartec 100 is an expedition-weight underwear. Polartec 200 is the most practical weight for casual fleece jackets and sweaters and Polartec 300 is the bulky expedition weight of fleece used for extreme winter clothing.

**Polyester** A versatile material that absorbs only 0.5 percent of its weight in moisture, making it an ideal underwear first-layer fabric, especially when combined with Lycra for stretch.

**Polycotton** This is a blend of cotton (35 percent) and polyester (65 percent), and provides a soft feel for sleeping-bag liners and clothing, without sacrificing too much water absorbency.

**Power stretch** This is an engineered fleece, shaved and blended with Lycra and designed not to pill. It can be used to create an ideal active-wear garment material.

**Ripstop nylon** Cross-woven threads running at right angles to each other "stop" a tear from advancing in nylon and other lightweight materials. Also comes in a diamond ripstop pattern.

**Shock-corded aircraft aluminum poles** To get maximum strength and flexibility for tent poles, you need a pole grade of 7075. One-eighth-inch elastic shock cord should run down the center of each pole to allow for ease of set up.

**Two-way zippers** Some zippers will have one zipper pull and a stop on the bottom. Two-way zippers will have a second zipper pull at the bottom of the jacket instead of a stop, allowing you to open the zip from the bottom for greater movement or venting.

**Waterproof-breathable coatings** Many manufacturers have developed waterproof-breathable coatings for fabrics. These allow creation of garments that can keep moisture out but still allow water vapor to escape. The limitations of these fabrics are in the washing: How many times can you wash the garment before the coating wears off? Check your garment's warranty.

# Suggested reading

A visit to your local Chapters bookstore, library or Web site will introduce you to a large selection of titles with more detailed knowledge about the wilderness. Here are few to start you off.

### Wilderness medicine

- *Medicine for the Outdoors*, by Paul Auerbach, MD, Little, Brown, 1986.
- *Wilderness Medicine*, by William Forgey, I.C.S. Books, 1987.
- *A Comprehensive Guide to Wilderness and Travel Medicine*, Adventure Medical Kits, by Eric Weiss, MD, 1997.

### Cold weather survival

- *Secrets of Warmth*, by Hal Weiss, Rocky Mountain Books, 1992.
- *Hypothermia, Frostbite and Other Cold Injuries*, by James A Wilkerson, Douglas McIntyre, 1986.
- *Outdoor Survival Skills*, by D. Larry Olsen, Chicago Review Press, 1997.

### Survival techniques

- *Down But Not Out*, R.C.A.F., Queen's Printer, 1970.
- *Bear Attacks: Their Causes and Avoidance*, by Steve Herrero, University of Calgary Press, 1992.

### Nature identification

- Audubon Field Guides, (various titles), Random House Canada.
- Animal Tracking and Behavior, by Donald and Lillian Stokes, Little, Brown, 1986.

### Weather and navigation

- *All about Weather*, by John Hulbert, Carousel Books, 1973.
- *Be an Expert with Map and Compass*, by Bjorn Kjellstrom, Simon & Schuster, 1994.

### Equipment

- *Product catalogues,* by Patagonia, North Face, Jack Wolfskin, Sierra Designs.
- *The Essential Outdoor Gear Manual*, by Annie Getchell, Ragged Mountain Press, 1995.

### Cooking

- *Dutch Oven Cookbook*, by Sheila Mills, Ragged Mountain Press, 1997.
- *Wanapitei Canoe Tripping Cookbook*, by Carol Hodgins, Highway bookshop, 1982.
- *Black Feather Guides Cookbook*, by Wally Schaber, (ed.), Trailhead (Ottawa), 1999.

### General reading

- *Path of the Paddle*, by Bill Mason, Van Nostrand, Reinhold, 1980.
- *Song of the Paddle*, by Bill Mason, Key Porter Books
- *Endangered Spaces*, by Monte Hummel, Key Porter Books, 1989.
- *Arctic Dreams*, by Barry Lopez, Scribner's, 1986.
- *The New Wilderness Handbook*, by Paul Petzoldt, Norton, 1984.

# OVER 100 CLASSIC COLES NOTES ARE ALSO AVAILABLE:

## SHAKESPEARE

- Antony and Cleopatra
- Antony and Cleopatra
  Questions & Answers
- As You Like it
- Hamlet
- Hamlet in Everyday English
- Hamlet – Questions & Answers
- Julius Caesar
- Julius Caesar in Everyday English
- Julius Caesar
  Questions & Answers
- King Henry IV – Part 1
- King Henry V
- King Lear
- King Lear in Everyday English
- King Lear – Questions & Answers
- Macbeth
- Macbeth in Everyday English
- Macbeth – Questions & Answers
- Measure for Measure
- Merchant of Venice
- Merchant of Venice
  in Everyday English
- Midsummer Night's Dream
- Midsummer Night's Dream in
  Everyday English
- Midsummer Night's Dream
  Questions & Answers
- Much Ado About Nothing
- Othello
- Othello – Questions & Answers
- Richard II
- Richard III
- Romeo and Juliet
- Romeo and Juliet
  in Everyday English
- Romeo and Juliet
  Questions & Answers
- Taming of the Shrew
- Tempest
- Twelfth Night

## SHAKESPEARE TSE*

- Hamlet T.S.E.
- Julius Caesar T.S.E.
- King Henry IV – Part I T.S.E.
- King Lear T.S.E.
- Macbeth T.S.E.
- Merchant of Venice T.S.E.
- Othello T.S.E.
- Romeo and Juliet T.S.E.
- Taming of the Shrew T.S.E.
- Tempest T.S.E.
- Twelfth Night T.S.E.
  *Total Study Edition

## LITERATURE AND POETRY

- Animal Farm
- Brave New World
- Catch 22
- Catcher in the Rye, Nine Stories
- Chrysalids, Day of the Triffids
- Crucible
- Death of a Salesman
- Diviners
- Duddy Kravitz and Other Works
- Edible Woman
- Emma
- Fahrenheit 451
- Farewell to Arms
- Fifth Business
- Glass Menagerie
- Grapes of Wrath
- Great Expectations
- Great Gatsby
- Gulliver's Travels
- Heart of Darkness
- Huckleberry Finn
- Iliad
- Jane Eyre
- King Oedipus, Oedipus at Colonus
- Lord of the Flies
- Lord of the Rings, Hobbit
- Man for All Seasons
- Mayor of Casterbridge
- 1984
- Odyssey
- Of Mice and Men
- Old Man and the Sea
- One Flew Over the Cuckoos Nest
- Paradise Lost
- Pride and Prejudice
- Machiavelli's The Prince
- Scarlet Letter
- Separate Peace
- Stone Angel and Other Works
- Street Car Named Desire
- Surfacing
- Tale of Two Cities
- Tess of the D'Urbervilles
- To Kill a Mockingbird
- Two Solitudes
- Who Has Seen the Wind
- Wuthering Heights

## THE CANTERBURY TALES

- The Canterbury Tales
- Prologue to the Canterbury Tales
  Total Study Edition
- Prologue to the Canterbury Tales
- French Verbs Simplified

## HOW TO GET AN A IN ...

- Calculus
- Permutations, Combinations &
  Probability
- School Projects & Presentations
- Senior Algebra
- Senior English Essays
- Senior Physics
- Sequences & Series
- Statistics & Data Analysis
- Trigonometry & Circle Geometry

## BIOLOGY

- Biology Notes

## CHEMISTRY

- Elementary Chemistry Notes Rev.
- How to Solve Chemistry Problems
- Introduction to Chemistry
- Senior Chemistry Notes Rev.

## MATHEMATICS

- Elementary Algebra Notes
- Secondary School Mathematics 1
- Secondary School Mathematics 4

## PHYSICS

- Elementary Physics Notes
- Senior Physics

## REFERENCE

- Dictionary of Literary Terms
- Effective Term Papers and Reports
- English Grammar Simplified
- Handbook of English Grammar &
  Composition
- How to Write Good Essays & Critical
  Reviews
- Secrets of Studying English

## Check the following stores:

## CHAPTERS
## COLES
## SMITHBOOKS
## WORLDS' BIGGEST BOOKSTORE

for our selection.